DESIGN YOUR BUSINESS MODEL

A must for startups

ABHIRAM TINKU

TABLE OF CONTENT

PREFACE

Being valuable is the most important ingredient of any writing work.

Unless a book is valuable to the reader, it is useless. It does not matter how persuasive it is, how organized the contents are or how clear the word conveys the ideas. This book is particularly useful for all those people who are somehow connected with business or want to know how a business model works.

This book is about business model design. It explains all the components of the business model, whether a startup or a large organization. Once an organization grows, it becomes more complicated but the core of all the businesses carries the same kind of nucleus which carries the same type of components.

Traditionally we believe, there are no free lunches in business. If a business is making your life easier, they will charge a fee for that. Have you ever surprised how some companies are giving you great value, without charging any fee? For example, a search engine helps you find any piece of information, without charging you. Of course, you pay for the internet, but not for the search engine. The money you pay for internet data is not going to search engine companies. These search engine companies are having an army of computer programmers to write programs and algorithm, to make the search very fast and most relevant. In doing so they are having a huge cost. They are paying millions of dollars as salary to their employees, they maintain a huge infrastructure. Is not it a magic, they have such a huge cost to help us search efficiently and they are not charging us a penny? Have you ever wondered "how does search engine make money when it doesn't charge even a penny?" This is a magic of the Business Model.

There's a famous quote related to this digitized world.

'If you aren't paying for it, you're the product'

This is the case with search engines, you help it make money by attracting advertisers. Their innovative business model makes revenue from advertiser rather than users and these companies are very successful in business.

Some businessman complains saying, how these e-commerce companies can sell products at such a low cost. Their finished product selling cost is even lower than the raw material cost of a common businessman.

Again, this magic relates to the business model. They took advantage of economies of scale. They innovated a complete supply chain, including no big inventory, no physical infrastructure, no floor managers so and so. There are many such examples of business models, evolving day by day.

In a business model, you have some building blocks which are basic to all the business. You can play with them, innovate the interconnection of those building blocks. Do the experiments on those building blocks. You can disrupt the industry by working on your business model. You can diagnose the situation by comparing the business model of yours and your competitor's business model.

If you don't improve the way you doing business, your competitors will eat you soon. Now the question is how to improve continuously? If you are working on a product only, after some years it's very difficult to improve it when it is already refined. In a business model, you have many ingredients to work on. You can also work on the integration of different sets of some of the ingredients. You can also improve the integration of all of these ingredients. Here you have a lot of combinations to play with and improve on those things. I have put some case studies in this book. You will see in our case studies; just a tweak in the business model can make your profit double or triple. This book is also worth reading for those who want to understand how business works in a logical sense.

I extend my gratitude to my family, friends and all those people who supported me throughout this writing work. Especially to my wife - *Preeti*. This book is also inspired by available information in public domain and other written work on business topics. Many examples, stories, anecdotes are the result of a collection from various sources, such as newspapers, magazines, blogs over the last 10 years. Unfortunately, sources were not always noted or available; hence it became impractical to provide wish to express my gratitude to those who may have contributed to this work, even though anonymously.

CHAPTER 1

TRUST

Trust is the most important thing in any relationship.

Trustworthiness is the reciprocal belief that another person will consider how his/her intentions and behaviors affect you. In the business world, Brand is now more important than ever. But what do we mean by BRAND? It is nothing but trust. Especially when it comes to relationships with clients, customers, employees and all stakeholders in your business. Having trust in someone is putting yourself vulnerable to someone, believing that assured reliance on the integrity of character, ability, strength or truth of someone or something. Trust is a strategically critical issue in any type of relationship because a relationship without trust is not a relationship at all. Over the long run, success in business is directly proportional to the network of positive relationships.

Trust is a key component of our social life. Our economy works because people trust each other and keep their commitments. Trust is the natural result of consistency in thousands of tiny actions, words, thoughts, and intentions. Trust does not happen all at once; gaining trust takes time. It might take years of caring and high-quality delivery to a certain client to fully gain their comfort and trust.

Due to the growing importance of trust in the business world today, now most of the organization and its leaders are giving it the focus and nurturing it deserves. Lack of trust causes a stressful, divisive atmosphere in a company. Trust is a non-negotiable aspect of a high-performing team, raising this awareness is only the starting point to building and sustaining trust. People who are supposed to be working together as a team need the team to truly function as such— not just in name, but also in spirit. To help team members connect on a human level and to forge supportive, meaningful relationships that produce results. That takes trust. Trust in one another. One can argue that the sole purpose of marketing and communications is to earn and nurture awareness and trust in the Brand.

To build team trust, people need to understand how trust works in teams—and to extend compassion to the

complexities and challenges that naturally come with it. They need to know where trust stands in their team, and be prepared to embrace opportunities to learn, grow and develop and to live the conviction trust-building takes. They need to be prepared to rebuild trust whenever it gets compromised.

Business strategists have developed a system with which they teach leaders, how to build the Eight Pillars of Trust:

- *Clarity* – People trust the vivid and mistrust the ambiguous.
- *Compassion* – People believe in those who care beyond themselves.
- *Character* – People notice those who go for what is right over what is easy.
- *Competency* – People have confidence in those who are confident and competent.
- *Commitment* – People believe in those who keep their promise and stand through adversity.
- *Connection* – People want to work with, do business and be around friends.
- *Contribution* – People believe I action and results.
- *Consistency* – People trust consistency over the time in the little things done.

The clarity in communication is important for making an impact. The clarity in job role improves the performance of employee on job. Clarity is also linked with rational. When someone sees clarity in something, he looks at it as a logical observer and he finds it aligned with his logical sense and belief. Sometimes we just "cannot understand" each other because we are too different in our perspectives, goals, experiences, and skills. Hence clarity also depends on how familiar it is for that person. It is often seen that the common ground used to connect people faster than anything. Speaking the same language, sharing the same social background are some examples for the same.

Compassion means "to suffer together." compassion involves allowing ourselves to be moved by suffering and experiencing the motivation to help alleviate and prevent it. An act of compassion is defined by its helpfulness. Qualities of compassion are patience and wisdom; kindness and perseverance; warmth and resolve. Compassion is not the same as empathy or altruism, though the concepts are related. While empathy refers more generally to our ability to take the perspective of and feel the emotions of another person, compassion is when those feelings and thoughts include the desire to help. That is why compassion makes us more trustworthy in the eyes of others.

The attribute we first associate with trustworthy behavior is integrity. Integrity means being predictable. This crucial aspect of good character is demonstrated through scrupulous honesty and moral courage. If we want people to trust us or our organization, they must believe that we will consistently do the right thing, regardless of the circumstances or pressures. Walk the talk is one of important ingredient which constitutes to the integrity. A leader who doesn't has the trust of his subordinates will never be able to achieve any target.

Other aspects of character include accountability and fairness. People trust those who accept responsibility for their choices and don't palm off blame to others. It's also important to be regarded as fundamentally fair.

But in business, confidence in character is not enough to justify trust. Trust also involves the conviction that the person or organization will successfully do what is expected. This competency dimension of trust lies in ability, knowledge, and judgment as well as a belief that the person or organization will be reliable and responsive. Reliability is established through diligence and follow-through while responsiveness involves respectful communication and demonstrated concern.

Commitment is the connection between our values, intentions and our actions. A connection is the coming together of more than one element, while commitment is the giving of ourselves to what we most believe and want. It is the merging of our ideals and our being. We surrender to our ideals and live them with commitment.

Consistency is the final element of trust in the extent to which leaders walk their talk and do what they say they will do. People rate such a leader high in trust.

why consistency is important? Consistency ensures customer expectations are met around the quality of deliverables. It gives customers predictability of deliverables that allow them

Design your business model

to better plan programs – critical since our goal and measurement of success is always around customer outcomes

Psychological View of Trust development at a very early stage in a Child

The trust versus mistrust stage is the first stage of psychologist Erik Erikson's theory of psychosocial development, which occurs between birth and approximately 18 months of age. According to Erikson, the trust versus mistrust stage is the most important period in a person's life because it shapes our view of the world, as well as our personalities.

An Overview of the Trust Versus Mistrust Stage

This first stage of psychosocial development consists of:

- *Psychosocial Conflict:* Trust versus mistrust
- *Major Question*: "Can I trust the people around me?"
- *Basic Virtue*: Hope
- *Important Event(s):* Feeding

What Happens During This Stage?

It is during this initial stage of development that children learn whether they can trust the world. As you might deduce, it is the care they receive from their parents and other adults that's vital to forming this trust.

Because an infant is entirely dependent upon his or her caregivers, the quality of care that the child receives plays an important role in the shaping of the child's personality. During this stage, children learn whether they can trust the people around them. When a baby cries, does his caregiver attend to his needs? When he is frightened, will someone comfort him? When she is hungry, does she receive nourishment from her caregivers?

An infant's ability to communicate his or her needs are limited, so crying carries an important message. When a baby cries, some need should be met with a response from caregivers, whether it involves providing food, safety, a fresh diaper, or a comforting cuddle. By responding quickly and appropriately to an infant's cries, a foundation of trust is established.

When these needs are consistently met, the child will learn that he can trust the people who are caring for him. If, however, these needs are not consistently met, the child will begin to mistrust the people around him.

If a child successfully develops trust, he will feel safe and secure in the world. Caregivers who are inconsistent, emotionally unavailable, or reject the child contribute to feelings of mistrust in the children they care for. Failure to develop trust can result in fear and a belief that the world is inconsistent and unpredictable.

Erikson believed that these early patterns of trust or mistrust help control, or at least exert, a powerful influence over that individual's interactions with others for the rest of his life.

Those who learn to trust caregivers in infancy will be more likely to form trusting relationships with others throughout their lives, Erikson believed.

Consumer psychology is very similar to the babies. If you care properly, they trust you and trust other businesses as well.

A Story on trust

A Little boy and her mother were crossing a bridge. The mother was reasonably frightened, she asked her little son,

'Sweetheart, please hold my hand so that you don't fall into the river.'

The little boy said, 'No, Mom. You hold my hand.'

'What's the difference?' Asked the puzzled mother.

'There's a big difference,' replied the little boy. 'If I hold your hand and something happens to me, chances are that I may let your hand go. But if you hold my hand, I know for sure that no matter what happens, you will never let my hand go.'

In any relationship, the essence of trust is not in its bind, however in its bond. So, hold the hand of the one that loves you rather than expecting them to hold yours.

Design your business model

CHAPTER 2

BUSINESS MODEL

Business models are the recipe of business.

A business model describes the rationale of how an organization creates, delivers, and captures value. In *The New, New Thing*, Michael Lewis offers up the simplest of definitions for *business model* — "All it meant was how you planned to make money"

According to management guru Peter Drucker, "a business model is supposed to answer who your customer is, what value you can create/add for the customer and how you can do that at reasonable costs."

Thus, a business model is a description of the rationale of how a company creates, delivers and captures value for itself as well as the customer. If there are the following 3 things, there is a business:

- *Product or service:* what you sell
- *People willing to pay for it:* your customers
- *A way to get paid:* how you will exchange a product or service for money

The widespread use of business models came into existence with the advent of the personal computer which let people test and model the different components of a business. Successful business models before that were mostly created by accident and not by design. It's different for business plans and business strategies though.
Every business model intrinsically has three parts

- everything related to designing and manufacturing the product
- everything related to selling the product, from finding the right customers to distributing the product
- everything related to how the customer will pay and how the company will make money

Business model can help you get rich. The concept of getting rich is very simple. Don't misunderstand me, I am not saying Getting rich is easy. But the concept is so simple that it can be put in just one line:

"Buy cheaper and sell dearer"

The concept involves term Buy and sell, the business model must have some ingredient under the buy category and some under the sell category.

Joan Magretta says in "Why Business Models Matter," 'A business model has two parts: "Part one includes all the activities associated with making something: designing it, purchasing raw materials, manufacturing, and so on. Part two includes all the activities associated with selling something: finding and reaching customers, transacting a sale, distributing the product, or delivering the service.

If operational efficiency is not working for your business, sometimes changing your business model can make the business profitable. Having an innovative and brand-new business model can keep you out of the competition. Since your business model is brand new, the market is not familiar with that. Competitors first hesitate to accept any new model; they will take time to understand and accept. It will take time for the competition to catch your model and you will also get the benefit of being an early bird.

In business, the overarching goal is to create [long-term] shareholder value. There are two different approaches uses very different means to achieve that end.

The Inside-Out approach is guided by the belief that the inner strengths and capabilities of the organization will make the organization prevail. The Outside-In approach is instead guided by the belief that customer value creation, customer orientation, and customer experiences are the keys to success.

From an Outside-In approach, long-term shareholder value is a consequence of listening and providing value to customers and helping them get their jobs done better than

Design your business model

the competition while providing a seamless customer experience. The ideal organizational culture is market- and customer-oriented and the targeted customer segments – buyers as well as users – are the source of inspiration and development. There is also a strong belief that if the customers aren't satisfied with the solutions offered, the business will suffer, and the shareholder value will diminish.

With an Inside-Out approach to business, you would likely see the effective use of company resources and core competencies as the main driver of shareholder value. Inside-Out strategists believe that a company achieves greater efficiencies and adapts more quickly to changing circumstances with this approach.

As you start and grow a business it is important to spend time thinking about your business strategy. Think of the business strategy as your map — with it, you'll determine the direction of your business and what you want it to look like in the future.

Different Types of Business Models

There are various types of business models that most companies fall into. Many of those operating under the basic categories of the manufacturer, distributor, retail or franchise. To develop a successful business plan, you first need to determine which business model you would like to follow.

Subscription

If customer acquisition costs are high, this business model might be the most suitable option. This model lets you keep customers over a long-term contract and get recurring revenues from them through repeat purchases. Ex: Online Movie platforms.

Nickel-and-dime

In this model, the basic product provided to the customers is very cost-sensitive and hence priced as low as possible. For every other service that comes with it, a certain amount is charged. Ex: All low-cost air carriers.

Retail

A retail outlet purchases product from a distributor or wholesaler, and then sells those products to the public or corporate end-users. Most department stores, except larger chains, would be considered retail outlets. Many online retailers purchase through wholesalers and follow the retail outlet business model.

Franchise Model

The franchise business model is unlike the others because with a franchise you can be a manufacturer, distributor or retail outlet. The type of business model you follow depends on the business you purchase, but with the franchise business model, there is always the added element of the franchise company. Franchising also incorporates the main kinds of business models within its structure. Franchise Chat reports that you can purchase a franchise directly from the franchise company, or you can buy it from a master franchise distributor that is licensed to sell franchises in your region. Thus, you employ the manufacturer, distributor or retail outlet model within the franchise business model. Ex: Fast food chains for Pizza and Burger.

Manufacturer

A manufacturer takes raw materials and creates a product. This business model also applies to companies that assemble products from premade parts. For example, some computer companies would be considered a manufacturer because it assembles its computers from parts made by other companies. A manufacturer can choose to represent its products directly to its customers, or it can outsource sales to another company. Ex: Car manufacturers.

Distributor

A distributor buys products from manufacturers and resells them to retailers or the public. Example – Auto Dealerships.

Brick-and-mortar

Brick-and-mortar is a traditional business model where the retailers, wholesalers, and manufacturers deal with the customers face-to-face in an office, a shop, or a store that the business owns or rents.

e-Commerce

E-Commerce business model is an up-gradation of the traditional brick-and-mortar business model. It focuses on selling products by creating a webstore(website) on the internet.

Bricks-and-clicks

A company that has both an online and offline presence allows customers to pick up products from the physical stores while they can place the order online. This model gives flexibility to the business since it is present online for customers who live in areas where they do not have brick-and-mortar stores. Examples – Almost all apparel companies nowadays.

Of course, most companies do not operate on any one of these business models but rather on a combination of some

Freemium

This is one of the most common business models on the Internet. Companies offer basic services to the customers for free while charging a certain premium for extra add-ons.

So, there will be multiple plans with various benefits for different customers. Generally, the basic service comes with certain restrictions or limitations, such as in-app advertisements, storage restrictions, etc., which the premium plans shall not have. For example, the basic version of some online cloud store comes with 2 GB storage. If you want to increase that limit, you can move to the Pro plan and pay a premium of almost $9.99 a month for it. Some online image editors allow you to edit only a certain number of images in the free basic plan while an unlimited number of images in the paid plan. Online video storage company's free plan comes with ads while the premium (Red) plan has no ad interruption plus it has other benefits too. This model is one of the most adopted models for online companies because it is not only a great marketing tool but also a cost-effective way to scale up and attract new users.

Aggregator

Aggregator business model is a recently developed model where the company has an agreement with various service providers of a niche and sell their services under its brand. The money is earned as commissions. Examples – app-based taxi services, app-based hotel booking

Online Marketplace

Online marketplaces aggregate different sellers into one platform who then competes with each other to provide the same product/service at competitive prices. The marketplace builds its brand over different factors like trust, free and/or on-time home delivery, quality sellers, etc. and earns commission on every sale carried on its platform. Examples – 'e-commerce companies.'

Advertisement

Advertisement business models are evolving even more with the rise of the demand for free products and services on the internet. Just like the earlier times, these business models are popular with media publishers like video storage companies, etc. where the information is provided for free but are accompanied by advertisements that are paid for by identified sponsors.

Data Licensing / Data Selling

With the advent of the internet, there has been an increase in the amount of data generated upon the users' activities over the internet. This has led to the advent of a new business model – the data licensing business model. Many companies like online massaging and blogging sell or license the data of its users or users of users to third parties which then use the same for analysis, advertising, and other purposes.

Agency-Based

An agency can be considered as a partner company which specializes in handling the non-core business activities like advertising, digital marketing, PR, ORM, etc. This company partners with several other companies that outsource their non-core tasks to them and is responsible to maintain privacy and efficiency in their work.

Design your business model

Affiliate Marketing

Affiliate marketing business model is a commission-based model where the affiliate builds its business around promoting a partner's product and directs all its efforts to convince its followers and users to buy the same. In return, the affiliate gets a commission for every sale referred to. An example of a business operating on the affiliate marketing business model is lifewire.com.

Dropshipping

Dropshipping is a type of e-commerce business model where the business owns no product or inventory but just a store. The actual product is sold by partner sellers who receive the order as soon as the store receives an order from the ultimate customer. These partner sellers then deliver the products directly to the customer.

Network Marketing

Network marketing or multi-level marketing involves a pyramid structured network of people who sell a company's products. The model runs on a commission basis where the participants are remunerated when –

- They make a sale of the company's product.
- Their recruits make a sale of the product.

Network marketing business model works on direct marketing and direct selling philosophy where there are no retail shops but the offerings are marketed to the target market directly by the participants. The market is tapped by making more and more people part of the pyramid structure where they make money by selling more goods and getting more people on board.

Crowdsourcing

The crowdsourcing business model involves users to contribute to the value provided. This business model is often combined with other business and revenue models to create an ultimate solution for the user and to earn money. Examples of businesses using the crowdsourcing business model are Wikipedia etc.

Peer 2 Peer Catalyst/Platform

A P2P economy is a decentralized internet-based economy where two parties interact directly with each other to buy or sell goods or to conduct a transaction without the intervention of any third party. A P2P catalyst is a platform where these users meet. Examples of P2P platforms are online marketplace sites and apps.

Blockchain

The Blockchain is an immutable, decentralized, digital ledger. By design, a blockchain is resistant to modification of the data. It is "an open, distributed ledger that can record transactions between two parties efficiently and in a verifiable and permanent way". It is a digital database that no one owns but anyone can contribute to it. Many businesses are taking this decentralized route to develop their business models. Models based on blockchain are not owned or monitored by a single entity. Rather, they work on peer-to-peer interactions and record everything on a digital decentralized ledger.

SAAS, IAAS, PAAS

There are usually three models of cloud service to compare: Software as a Service (SaaS), Platform as a Service (PaaS), and Infrastructure as a Service (IaaS). Many companies have started offering their software, platform, and infrastructure as a service. The 'as a service' business model works on the principle of pay as you go where the customer pays for his usage of such software, platform, and infrastructure; he pays for what and how many features he has used and not for what he hasn't.

High Touch

The High Touch model is one which requires lots of human interaction. The relationship between the salesperson and the customer has a huge impact on the overall revenues of the company. The companies with this business model operate on trust and credibility. Examples – Hair salons, consulting firms.

Low Touch

The opposite of the High Touch model, the Low Touch model requires minimal human assistance or intervention in selling a product or service. Since as a company, you do not have to maintain a huge sales force, your costs decrease, though such companies also focus on improving technology

Design your business model

to further reduce human intervention while making the customer experience better at the same time. Ex: e-commerce company.

Shared Saving model

In this model, a proposition is made to save some targeted amount of money by increasing operational/innovative efficiency. The business or agency then charge a fee as a percentage of any net savings realized as a result of their efforts.

Leasing business model

Leasing refers to renting large or high-profile items like machines and electronic equipment instead of them selling it.

Product as a service

Product as a service means to sell the service of a product rather than selling the actual product. Like online taxi services

Pay as Go (Utility) Business Model

The business model charges as per the usage of the product or service.

Example: This model includes electricity, water, and cell phone companies

Of course, most companies do not operate on any one of these business models but rather on a combination of some. Like you can be a Bricks-and-clicks Low Touch Retailer or a High Touch Subscription-Based Manufacturer. What business model you choose depends on your business needs and what value you want to create for your stakeholders. For how much we love to believe that things can be easily classified. Complex Organizations have complex hybrid business models. For example, a hybrid business model as shown below.

The revenue stream of a Hybrid business model

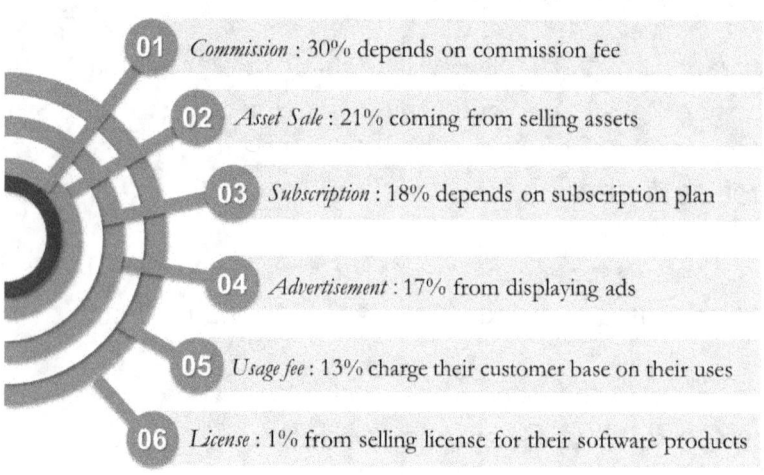

01 *Commission* : 30% depends on commission fee

02 *Asset Sale* : 21% coming from selling assets

03 *Subscription* : 18% depends on subscription plan

04 *Advertisement* : 17% from displaying ads

05 *Usage fee* : 13% charge their customer base on their uses

06 *License* : 1% from selling license for their software products

Thus, rather than rely on a single type of model, they are dependent on the mixture of those models. The way those models interact is quite subtle, yet that is what creates, unlocks and generates value in the long-term.

Design your business model

Next, we will see how to develop the perfect business model for your startup, so that the chances of your success are amplified.

A story on Business Model

Once upon a time, two ambitious young friends named Mike and John lived in a small village. The young men had big dreams. They had a dream to become the richest men in the village. All they needed was an opportunity. One day that opportunity arrived. The villagers decided to hire two men to carry water from a nearby river to a cistern in the town square. The job went to Mike and John. Each man grabbed two buckets and headed to the river. By the end of the day, they had filled the town cistern to the brim. The village elder paid them some money for each bucket of water. They were happy with the earning opportunity. Some days passed like this.

Mike got an idea after working for some routine days. He told his friend John "Instead of carrying buckets back and forth for pennies a day, why can't we build a pipeline from the village to the river." John looked at Mike "A pipeline! Whoever heard of such a thing?" John shouted. "We've got a great job, Mike. By the end of the week, I can buy a new pair of shoes. By the end of the month a cow. By the end of six months, I can buy a new hut. We're set for life! Get out of here with your pipeline." Mike Continued his idea. He would work part of the day carrying buckets, and part of the day and weekends building his pipeline.

One day Mike realized his pipeline was half-way finished, which meant he only had to walk half as far to fill his buckets! Mike used the extra time to work on his pipeline. Finally, Mike's big day arrived, his pipeline was complete! The villagers crowded around as the water gushed from the pipeline into the village cistern! Now that the village had a steady supply of freshwater, people from around the countryside moved into the village and the village prospered. Once the pipeline was complete, Mike didn't have to carry buckets anymore. The water flowed whether he worked or not. It flowed while he ate. It flowed while he slept. It flowed on weekends while he played. The more the water flowed into the village, the more money flowed into Mike's pockets.

Once the pipeline started working, Mike prospered while his friend John got jobless immediately.

Change made in the channel of product delivery made a huge impact in business and profit of Mike. Channel of delivery is a core ingredient of a business model. You can see here, how a small change in business model make a huge impact.

A ship in harbor is safe, but that is not what ships are built for

People think why they should take the stress, time and effort to build pipelines when things are going fine. They say they deserve to relax in the recliner and watch TV after a hard day work. Got a few bucks in the bank.... kids are doing good in school........... no need to "rock the boat". Life is short, enjoy the life and live with peace.

There is a contrary view: life is not meant for being still, calm and relaxed but life is meant for adventure and to have more and intense experiences. After death there is complete piece, so act and take the risk until you are alive.

It is said 'A ship in harbor is safe, but that is not what ships are built for'

CHAPTER 3

BUSINESS MODEL CANVAS

Business model canvas is a great tool to understand a business in a straightforward, structured way.

Business model canvas is like a checklist if we have put all ingredients in the business recipe for an awesome taste. Business model canvas is like solving a mathematical problem or numerical problems of physics. In such situations, we used to have certain formulas and postulates, which sets boundary for solving problems. Business model canvas is presenting a control system of a business. If a business is not doing well, it can be reviewed with the help of this canvas to find out what gone wrong. This canvas is also useful to check if the business plan is having any big error. In my opinion: If we describe the business model canvas in one line, it is a template for a good business plan.

The Business Model Canvas was proposed by *Alexander Osterwalder* in his earlier work on Business Model Ontology. Since the release of Osterwalder's work in 2008, many new canvases for specific niches are Ubiquitous in business world.

This canvas can describe any company on a single sheet of paper, whether it is the largest company of the world or a newly formed small startup.

Why the Business model canvas?

- Easy to understand
- Easy to communicate
- Shows connections
- Focused
- Flexible
- Customer-focused

Business model Canvas building blocks

Key Activities	Value Proposition	Customer Segment
Key Resources	Start Here	Customer relationship
Key Partners		Delivery Channels
Cost Structure		Revenue Stream

1. Key partners

   - Who are your key partners/suppliers?
   - What are the motivations for the partnerships?

2. Key activities
   - What key activities strengthen your value proposition?
   - What activities are important the most in distribution channels, customer relationships, revenue streams…?

3. Value proposition
   - What core value do you intended to deliver to the customer?
   - Which customer needs are you satisfying?

4. Customer relationship

- What type of relationship you establish with the target customer?
- How can you integrate that into your business in terms of format?

5. Customer segment
    - Which classes are you creating values for?
    - Who is your most important customer?

6. Key resource
    - What key resources you need to deliver your value proposition?
    - What resources are important the most in distribution channels, customer relationships, revenue streams...?

7. Distribution channel
    - Which channel of delivery suits you and your customers in cost and format?
    - Which channels work best? Which channel customer expect you to approach. How can they be integrated into your and your customers' and suppliers' routines?

8. Cost structure
    - What is the most cost in your business?
    - Which key activities/resources are the most cost sensitive?

9. Revenue stream

- Which is the most effective value, your customers willing to pay for?
- What and how do they recently pay? How would they prefer to pay?
- Which revenue streams generate the most of revenue? How many revenue streams contribute to the overall revenues?

Let us see some examples of business models strategy, explained on canvas

The business model for a Blade and Razor

A business model which involves selling an item at a low price, sometimes even at a loss, to sell complementary or consumable products later. The name refers to sell hand-held razors at low cost and then make a high margin of profit by selling the replaceable blades. The pricing and marketing strategy are designed to generate reliable, recurring income by locking a consumer onto a platform or proprietary tool for a long period.

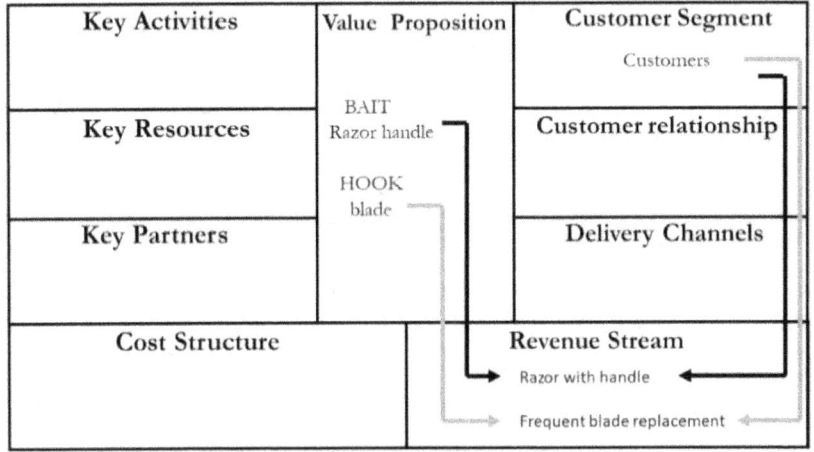

Key Activities	Value Proposition	Customer Segment
		Customers
Key Resources	BAIT Razor handle	Customer relationship
	HOOK blade	
Key Partners		Delivery Channels
Cost Structure		Revenue Stream
		Razor with handle
		Frequent blade replacement

The business model for online video calling app

Having a free product makes it easy to get customers and internet economics makes this very attractive because the marginal cost of every new free user will be very low. Free users can also be good marketing because even though a free user might not convert, they can invite other free users who might. Free video call on the internet invites a lot of customers. Very few of them also call on phones, they will use the paid service which is also cheap compared to traditional phone to phone calls.

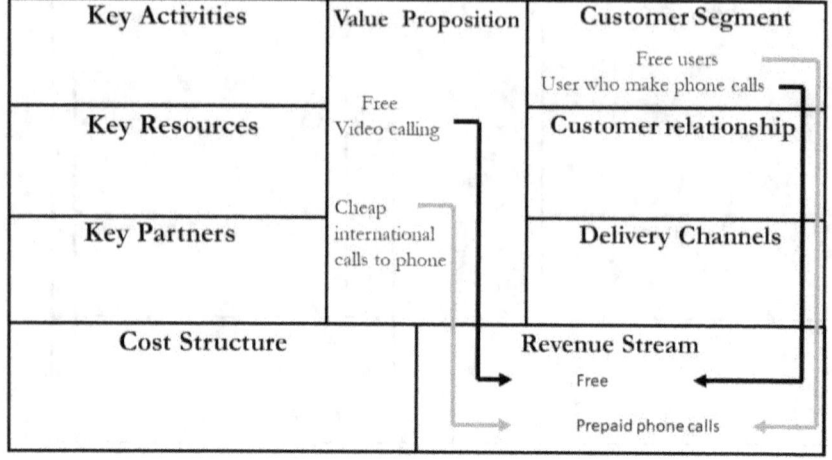

Key Activities	Value Proposition	Customer Segment
		Free users
		User who make phone calls
Key Resources	Free Video calling	Customer relationship
Key Partners	Cheap international calls to phone	Delivery Channels
Cost Structure		Revenue Stream
		Free
		Prepaid phone calls

The concept is similar to the "freemium," in which products and services (Apps, email, games, etc.) are given away for free with the expectation of making money later on upgraded services or added feature.

Value Proposition

According to experts, 72% of all new product innovations flop. It is not because the products had flaw in its design, quality, marketing, pricing or sells force. Reason to flop was the value proposition. It's not about the product you made, but it's about the product solving customers' problems or improves their situation. Value is created when a person makes something useful for the society and shares it with the needful. It is the customer who has the last word on the products value proposition. It's not about how good a product is but how useful a customer finds it and ready to pay for it.

Design your business model

Not everything that you are passionate about or skilled in is interesting to the rest of the world, and not everything is marketable. I can be very passionate about watching TV, but no one is going to pay me to do it. Likewise, any person won't be able to provide a solution to every problem or be interesting to everyone. But in the overlap between the two ellipses, where passion or skill meets usefulness, a microbusiness built on common ground and value can thrive. We do have skills which we like, and the world is also interested in that, we can focus on those skills to create value for the world. In simple formula;

Passion or skill + usefulness = value

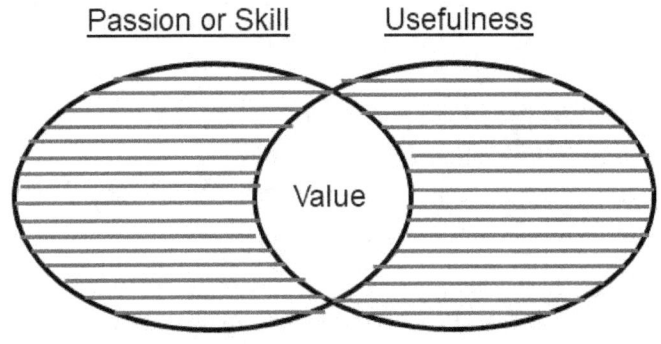

The easiest definition of value would be: Value means helping people.

A value proposition stands as a promise by a company/organization to a customer or customer segment. The proposition is an easy-to-understand reason why a customer should buy that specific product or service from that company. A value proposition should clearly explain how that specific product fulfills a need, communicate the specifics of its added benefit, and state the reason why it's better than similar products on the market. The ideal value proposition is simple and to-the-point and appeals to a customer's strongest decision-making drivers. According to experts, "a value proposition statement should consist of four parts: capability, impact, proof, and the price customer is expected to pay.

In short, a value proposition is a clear statement that

- Explains how your product is relevant to the required need. How it solves customers' problems or improves their situation.

- Delivers unique and specific benefits.

- Tells the ideal customer why they should buy from you and not from the competitor.

- While writing a value proposition come in various forms, a basic formula includes four parts:

  i. A headline
  ii. A sub-headline
  iii. A list of key benefits
  iv. An image

On the business model canvas left side three items are about value creation and the right side three items are about value delivery. In the central, there is value proposition.

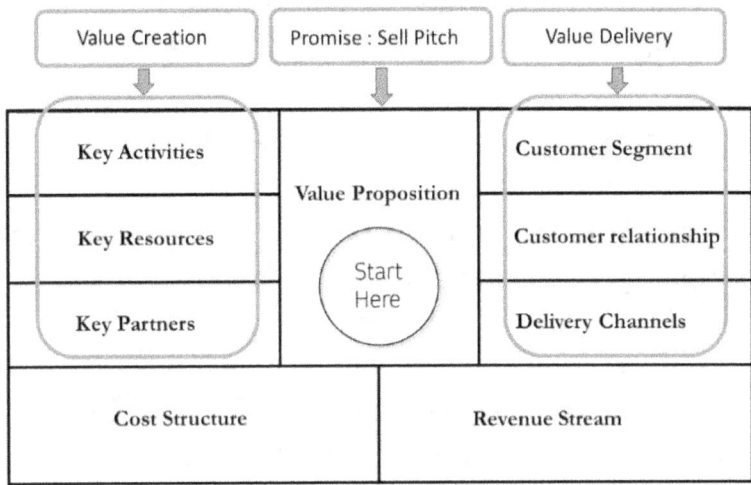

Following are three main components in the value creation network:

Key partners

The companies use the resources, knowledge, and capabilities of their partners to perform. The most important partners that a company can have are the owners, employees, suppliers, the government, the institutions, etc.

It can be useful to differentiate among three motivations for creating partnerships:

Optimization and economy of scale: This most basic form of partnership or buyer-supplier relationship is designed to

Design your business model

optimize the allocation of resources and activities. It is not wise for a company to own all resources or perform every activity by itself. Optimization and economy of scale partnerships are usually formed to reduce costs, and often involve outsourcing or sharing infrastructure and resources.

Reduction of risk and uncertainty: Partnerships can help reduce risk in a volatile and competitive environment. It is usual for competitors to form a strategic alliance in one area while competing in another. Blu-ray, for example, is an optical disc format jointly developed by a group of the world's leading consumer electronics, personal computers, and media manufacturers. The group cooperated to bring Blu-ray technology to market, yet individual members compete in selling their Blu-ray products.

Acquisition of resources and activities: Few big companies, who own all the resources or perform all the activities described by their business models. Rather, they extend their capabilities by relying on other firms to furnish resources and perform certain activities. Such partnerships can be motivated by the needs to acquire knowledge, licenses, or customer access. A mobile phone manufacturer, for example, may license a popular operating system for its handsets rather than developing one in-house. An insurer may choose to rely on independent brokers to sell its policies instead of developing its own sales force.

Design your business model

Key activities

Key activities are the activities that needed to be done to create a value proposition for the customers from the available resources. It shows all the crucial activities and links between the company and its partners that are necessary to create value for the customers. You should look at your value proposition. What are the key things that you need to do to have control over your value proposition? If you are a florist you need to buy the flowers, prepare them and deliver them. You also need to manage your promotional channels and customer relations, so that customers come to the shop.

If outrun a plastics factory your key activities are likely to revolve about maintaining production, keeping the operations safe and working out how to reduce costs and improve productivity to keep pace with market changes. Here there are many more things that you could be doing. Key activities are the critical things that you absolutely must do to develop and maintain your competitive advantage.

- o Key activities can be divided as:

    - a) Internal key activities are the activities that are made inside the organization
    - b) External key activities are the relations between the organization and its partners

How to find your key activity

What's the most important activities to build your product or service?

- What's most important to distribute your product and service?
- What kinds of activities are important to maintain customer relationships? (Personal Service, Your Office, Sharing Experience, etc.)
- What kinds of activities are important to your revenue streams? (Credit Limit, Fast Payment, Trust, etc.)

Typical key activities include Research & Development, Production, Marketing, sales and customer service, etc.

Key resources

These are the main assets that are needed in the process of adding value to the product or process for the customers. Most of the business requires these 4 key resources to run a business.

Physical: Manufacturing facilities, buildings, vehicles, machines are examples of Physical Resources. The Physical resources are often capital intensive. For example, MacDonald's has an enormous global network of stores, storage buildings, IT infrastructure and logistics infrastructure.

Intellectual: Brand value, proprietary knowledge, patents and copyrights, partnerships, and customer databases are Intellectual Resources. These are really important for a strong business model.

Microsoft and SAP rely heavily on software and related intellectual property, which are developed over many years. Google's intellectual resources are the algorithms and of course the brand name, it has developed over the years. For Nike, its numerous patents, and trademarks. Nike Air is an example of intellectual resource.

Human: Undoubtedly, human resources are the most important resources required to run a business. Every enterprise requires human resources, but people are particularly prominent in certain high touch kind of business models. For example, human resources are crucial in knowledge-intensive and creative industries like schools, Consultancies, advertisement agency, and hospitals which cannot operate without human resources.

Financial: Business requires financial resources to carry out the business. These resources are cash, bank deposits, investments like stocks and bonds.

You can see already; key resources contribute to a large part of your overall cost. Proper balancing of this helps you estimate a break-even point. Any guess on what are the other parts of the overall cost?

Can you now think of all the key resources that your business requires? Which key resource do you think plays the most crucial role in your business? How this will affect the cost structure of your company?

Following are three main components in value delivery network:

Customer relationship

Customer satisfaction has important implications for the economic performance of firms because it can increase customer loyalty and usage behavior and reduce customer complaints and the likelihood of customer defection

There can be two distinguished attributes of a developed relationship between supplier and customer:

Trust: Trust means confidence, reliability and security in any relationship and can be treated as the biggest investment in building long term relationships. Trust is developed between the two parties when they experience flawless and satisfying motives between each other. As a result of knowing more about each other, all the doubts and risks are minimized and lead to inevitably smooth business. Lack of trust, on the other hand, weakens the relationship by damaging the foundation. Chances of uncertainty and conflicts increases.

Commitment: Commitment is yet another milestone that guaranty a long-term mutual relationship. Commitment can only be attained when there is mutual trust and the two parties respect each other's values. In a committed relationship, both suppliers and customers strive to uphold the relationship and don't want to exit which in turn results in building the relationship stronger and sharper. There is, in fact, a huge cost which is incurred in switching from committed relationships of one supplier and build new relationships with other suppliers from scratch.

How to build better customer relationships?

Understand what your customers value: To find out what your customers value the most, always listen to what they say and how they say it—and adjust your approach to match their expectations.

Some people would like a lot of personal contact with your business. Others may not be interested in getting too much attention: They just want to call you up, place an order and get on their day. Some will be very price-conscious, some quality perfectionist, while others will be looking for all the bells and whistles. Do your best to keep listening!

Show you genuinely care: As a rule, people want to connect beyond the professional level. That's why it pays off to be friendly and personal. Find out what you have in common with customers and engage on that; follow up on key details; ask about their kids or wish them a happy birthday on the day.

Some people naturally retain those kinds of details by their behavior, but if you don't, just write them down in your contact list. The key is to always be authentic. "Customers can tell when you aren't being genuine," experts say, "If being a 'people person' isn't your strong skill, think about hiring someone who is."

Adapt to their pace: If a customer picks up the phone and is clearly in a hurry, respect his time, don't slow them down with small talk and pleasantries. But if a customer calls and wants to chat, make sure you don't rush them off the phone.

Let your brand be your guide: Your branding and marketing make a promise about customer experience and your organization as a whole—and it's essential to deliver that, what is promised. If you claim you're always there for customers but people can't get beyond your voicemail when they call you, then you've failed to keep your promise.

The promises you need to keep are closely related to your organization's unique value proposition. Think of a membership-based wholesale retailer and a boutique, high-end technology shop. While the customer experience could not be any more different—a big warehouse versus personal, attentive service—both are delivering exactly what their customers expect to receive.

Make sure all your customer-facing employees are well trained on this. "Even if they have experience from somewhere else, they can't approach their job the same way," expert says. "They have to reflect the commitment, organization stands for."

Model the behavior you want to see: The way you treat your employees shows them how they're supposed to treat your customers. If you're always trying to cut costs, your employees may assume they shouldn't be offering discounts or adding value in other ways, which can go a long way toward exceeding customer expectations.

Remember that relationships are built over time:

Expert says that while it's important to go above and beyond, "You don't need to hit a home run with every conversation."

Some companies use customer relationship management (CRM) software to help manage their relationships over time. While these can be helpful, especially in larger businesses with formal customer relationship programs, they aren't necessary to deliver exceptional customer experiences.

"The most important thing is to be conscious of the experience you're delivering, and to deliver it consistently," says Palin.

Channel

A distribution channel represents a chain of businesses or intermediaries through which the final buyer purchases a good or service. Companies create a distribution path, a distribution chain or a distribution channel to get the product out of the factory, onto the physical location, but the price tag on it and the shelf, ready for the customer reach for it. Conversely, it also describes the pathway payments make

from the end consumer to the original vendor. Channels are broken into two different forms—direct and indirect.
A direct channel allows the consumer to make purchases from the manufacturer while an indirect channel allows the consumer to buy the good from distribution channels. A distributor channel includes wholesalers, retailers, distributors, and the Internet. Increasing the number of ways, a consumer can find a good can increase sales. The method of distribution should add value to the consumer at the same time business should look at cost-effective ways.

Direct sale: Direct distribution would mean that the manufacturer finds a way to directly communicate to customers without using any market intermediaries and will deliver the goods themselves.

Internet and E-commerce have popularized direct distribution, however, we find E-commerce is very specific and therefore we have allocated a special place for E-commerce at the bottom of this article.

The most important aspect of direct distribution marketing is communication to the end customer. You need to make sure you are sending the right message. It is also known as B to C, business to customer.

Brokers and distributors

If a manufacturer chose to work with agents and brokers, they decide to directly delegate part of their tasks to those Intermediaries. They act as an extension of the producer in the sense they represent them before the end customer.

Let us get the food industry for example.

Before contracting a broker, the food manufacturer would have to offer the stores the production themselves.

And that is usually the case with smaller vendors. However, as the business expands, they would look for alternatives for shipping their produce to the store.

That would be done by a broker to handle the sales, or a distributor, who would take care to ship the goods to shops in various locations.

Wholesalers/Retailers

Working with wholesalers and retailers is usually a preferred distribution chain link because wholesalers and retailers do purchase the product from the manufacturer and therefore, they take on the risk if the products do not sell well.

Working with resellers works perfectly for digital products.

E-Commerce changes the game of distribution

E-commerce completely changes the game of distribution for several reasons.

1. An e-commerce company, depending on their business model may see themselves as the manufacturer, a wholesaler, or a retailer. Those roles have become more fluid.
2. E-commerce in general immediately makes products available for a large customer base and therefore

fewer intermediaries are needed. Storage locations needs are limited, too.

3. With predictive and prescriptive analysis of big data, e-commerce makes it possible that inventory management and shipment are predicted in advance and optimized.

The decision you will take about your distribution channel will affect your pricing, your products, your relationships with your intermediaries and your customers.

Make sure you take your time and carefully think over your strategy in advance.

Only delegate when you are comfortable that a third party will do the job better at a lower ultimate cost.

Always consider E-commerce as a distribution channel. It can easily be diversified, it is the most profitable, and it can be used in addition to your other distribution efforts.

Customer segment

It is the process of dividing mass markets into groups with similar needs and wants. The rationale for segmentation is that to achieve competitive advantage and superior performance, firms should: "identify segments of industry demand, target specific segments of demand, and develop specific 'marketing mixes' for each targeted market segment ". It allows the business to focus on potential customers, where the demand for that particular product exists.

Why is Customer Segmentation Important?

For the modern marketer, customer segmentation isn't just a suggestion – it's a necessity.

We have many benefits of customer segmentation; it can allow your company to grow.

Improved Focus: The more you know about your customers, the better you'll be able to focus on catering to their needs. In doing so, you can fine-tune your product specifically to your customers' needs, making them feel as if you've created it just for them.

Furthermore, you can use segmentation data to create targeted advertising and marketing campaigns for subsets of customers, as well.

In either of these cases, segmentation increases the chances of targets becoming prospects, and prospects becoming customers. Without customer segmentation data, you're simply putting your product "out there" and hoping for the best.

Increased Competitiveness: Going along with that last sentiment, using customer segmentation strategies allows you to be active, assertive, and even aggressive when it comes to building your business.

(On the other hand, using the "spray and pray" method when creating advertising and marketing campaigns is rather passive, as you simply sit back and wait for customers to come to you.)

Once you know who your customers are, and you know what they're looking for, you can pursue them relentlessly. And, since you know exactly how your product or service will ease their pain points, you can be confident that your efforts will increase sales and revenue.

An increase in sales numbers and revenue, in turn, will result in your company owning a bigger slice of the market share in your industry.

Ability to Expand: As your company grows, it'll also be able to expand – in two different ways.

In the literal sense, you may be able to expand the physical area your company caters to. Customer segmentation allows you to do so strategically since you'll know to move into areas populated by individuals most similar to your current customer base.

Think of the popular 'app-based taxi' company. At first, it catered to individuals strictly within the San Francisco area. Once the company was financially prepared to expand, it began offering its services in other metropolitan areas across the country (rather than simply expanding outward from San Fran and beyond).

You also might expand your company in terms of the products or services you provide your customers, as well. Once your customers trust you to provide an effective solution to one of their major pain points, they'll be more likely to trust you when you introduce a solution to another one of their problems.

Perhaps the most ubiquitous example of a company expanding into a new market is a leading mobile phone manufacturer. What was once a company predominantly focused on producing computers is now a tech giant responsible for creating smartphones, smartwatches, and televisions. One of the main reasons it has been able to expand into various markets so seamlessly is because it knows what its customers want, and relentlessly works toward providing it for them.

By truly understanding your customers on an almost individual level, you'll have a better idea of how your company can expand its reach – in turn increasing its potential for growth.

Increased Customer Retention: As we've alluded to throughout this post, customer segmentation allows you to fine-tune the product or service you offer your customers to better suit their needs – in turn, increases their trust in your brand.

When your customers trust your company, they'll be more likely to return to you when they find themselves in a similar situation in the future. On the surface, this is because you've helped them out in the past, having given them exactly what they needed to overcome a certain pain point.

But it goes much deeper than that.

Proper customer segmentation allows you to stay connected to your customers even after you've made a sale.

By segmenting your customers into specific subsets, you gain a general idea of *what else* you can provide them (in addition to your main product) that will show them you're dedicated to helping alleviate their pain. In doing so, you make it much more likely that they'll return to you when they're in need some time down the line.

Capitalize When the Time is Right: Segmenting your customers also allows you to know when a specific persona is most likely to need your services.

Notice, though: we said, "a specific persona," and not "your entire customer base."

In other words, different types of customers will require your services at different times throughout the year.

For example, if your company sells chocolate and other assorted candies, you can assume demand will increase around holidays like Valentine's Day and Halloween.

But the people buying these products will not always be the same customer segment. During Valentine's Day, you'd likely create advertisements full of sentimental messages, while during Halloween you'd focus on creating spooky commercials aimed at children.

While its obvious to know that Halloween is an optimal time to market candy to kids, the point of this example is:

Design your business model

By having a well-rounded understanding of who your target customers are, you'll have a much better idea of when they'll be most likely to purchase your product.

Price Optimization: When you know where your customers stand in terms of financial and societal status, you'll be in a much greater position to offer your product or service at a price they consider reasonable.

By optimizing the price of your product, you not only ensure your customers get the most value for their dollar, but you also ensure your company generates the maximum amount of revenue possible.

We'll discuss this a little more in-depth later in this book when we talk about estimating the value of each of your customer segments in case studies. Here, just know the focus is on revenue generated – not sales numbers.

In nutshell, it goes like create value, make a proposition and sell the value to the right customer, who needs that value. This circle is closed here.
But it doesn't involve the main reason why the business is in the existence. The business must make profit to be in existence. Here comes the accounting. In the simplest term, profit is all about how much money is coming to the business and what are expanses. Business model canvas capture it in bottom two cells, which is cost structure and revenue stream.

Cost Structure

Cost structure refers to the types and relative proportions of fixed and variable costs that a business have. The concept can be defined in smaller units, such as based on-product, service, product line, customer, division, or geographic region. Cost structure is used as a tool to determine prices, if your pricing strategy is based on cost incurred, as well as to highlight areas in which costs might potentially be reduced or at least subjected to better control. Thus, the cost structure concept is mainly a management accounting concept; it has no applicability to financial accounting.

To define a cost structure, you need to define every cost incurred concerning a cost object. The following bullet points highlight key elements of the cost structures of various cost objects in a business:

- Product cost structure
- Fixed costs. Direct labor, manufacturing overhead
- Variable costs. Direct materials, commissions, production supplies, piece-rate wages

To maximize profits, businesses must find every possible way to minimize costs. While some fixed costs are vital to keeping the business running, a financial analyst should always review the financial statements to identify excessive expenses that do not provide any additional value to core business activities.

When an analyst gets into detail of the overall cost structure of a company, he/she can identify feasible cost reduction methods without affecting the quality of products sold or service provided to customers. The financial analyst should also keep a close eye on the cost trend of business to ensure stable cash flows and no sudden cost rise occurring.

Cost allocation is an important process for a business because if costs are misallocated, the business may get jeopardize by cost allocation in wrong heads which leads to wrong decisions to overprice/underprice a product or invest unnecessary resources in non-profitable products. Financial analyst has to make sure costs are correctly distributed to the destined cost objects and appropriate cost allocation are chosen.

Looking at Cost allocation an analyst can calculate the per-unit costs for different product lines, business units, or departments and thus, find out the profits per-unit. With this information, a financial analyst can provide insights on improving the profitability of certain products, replacing the least profitable products, or implementing strategies to reduce costs.

Example of cost structure

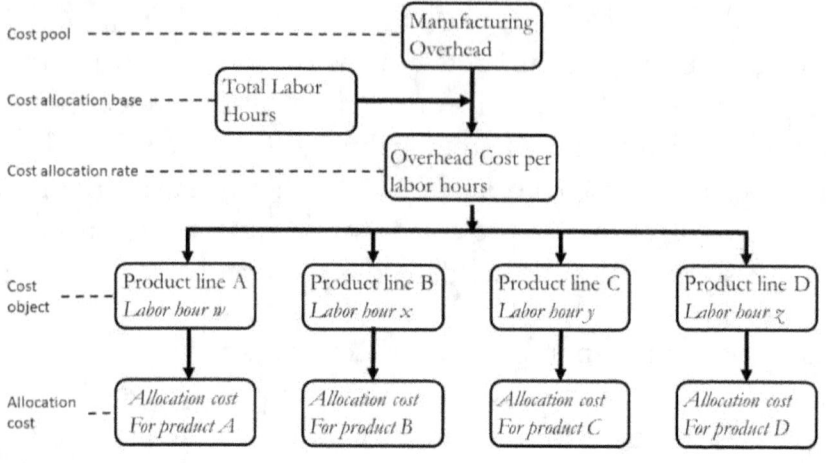

Revenue stream

The company's revenue stream is the amount of money that it receives from selling a particular product or service. Revenue is a Key Performance Indicator (KPI) for all businesses. If customers lies in the heart of your business model, Revenue Streams are its arteries. You must analyze, for what value is each Customer Segment truly willing to pay? Successfully answering that question allows your business to generate one or more Revenue Streams from each Customer Segment. Besides, maybe there are places you are leaving money on the table. Without knowing what other possible revenue streams there are, it's going to be hard to know if that's the case or not.

In short – look for the other way, how you can make money? Money isn't the sole consideration in business—but it's an important one. Ask following three questions for every idea:

- How this idea will generate revenue?
- How much revenue this idea will generate?
- Is there a way to generate more revenue stream and get paid more than once?

Revenue Streams can be generated in many different and innovative ways and you can use a mix of these different ways for your company:

1. Sale of physical product: The customer pays in cash for the product (for example, books, furniture…) and the customer is then free to do whatever she or he wants with it.
2. Usage fee: The customer pays a user fee for a particular service, such as water, phone, hotel room, etc. As such, the amount paid by the customer depending on how much of the service is being used (for example, how many liters of water, how many nights at the hotel, how many calls, etc.)
3. Subscription fee: The customer pays, for example, once a month, or yearly, for a particular service. For example, sports/gym facilities often use this option. Even if you do not use it, you pay. This could also work for products. You have your customers pay an

amount to you every month and in return, you deliver your product regularly.

4. Lending/renting/leasing: This Revenue Stream grants someone the right to use a particular product for a fixed period in return for a fee. This method can be used for rentals of cars, rentals of farm machinery, etc.

5. Brokerage fees: Through this Revenue Stream, your company gets its revenue from an intermediate service. This method is often used by real estate agents (earning a commission every time they match the buyer and seller) and credit card providers (getting a percentage of the value of each sale completed between the merchant and the customer).

6. Advertising: Your business may charge fees for advertising a product, service or brand. For example, newspapers and media rely on this method.

7. Volume and unit selling: Your company charges a fixed price for a product. However, if the customer chooses to buy your product in higher quantities, they could get a discount (either by a lower price or additional products). You can have different prices and discounts for different Customer Segments. For example, to encourage large purchases of apple, you give 2 free apples to every customer who buys more than 2 kg.

While a promotion strategy seems to be very attractive (giving out products/services for free), you should not use it as your main revenue model since customers get easily used to getting them for free and if you suddenly stop giving products/services away, your customers may leave you and move to your competitor.

Example of revenue stream:

Design your business model

CASE STUDIES

Design your business model

CHAPTER 4

THE BUSINESS MODEL OF AN ONLINE SEARCH ENGINE

The online search engine receives over 63,000 searches per second on any given day worldwide. That's the average figure of how many people use search engine per day, which translates into at least 2 trillion searches per year

Search engine algorithms are very dynamic - for the few major changes they publish, it makes thousands of tweaks and changes behind the scenes you never hear about.

Every search engine will tell you that algorithms are implemented to help match search queries with the best information possible. What they don't tell you is that they do this with a bias: they want to know what you are interested in to better deliver sponsored ads to you.

Websites show up in searches based on a wide variety of factors that involve everything from search engine optimization (SEO) to brand popularity in searches, social network mentions, videos, images, links to and from sites, and even factors like how many people select your site when it shows up in searches - and what they do once they get there.

It is no wonder that the industry of search engines spawned the industry of search engine optimization, which, in turn, gave birth to another industry: SEO scam artists.

Top search engines handle almost 1.2 trillion search queries per year and have partnered with over 2 million websites which have a reach to over 90% of people on the internet. Imagine advertising to such a huge market.

How Does Search Engine Make Money from Advertisements?

There are three components of the Search engine business model that aid Search engine to help advertise: AdWords, AdSense, and AdMob.

- AdWords is the advertiser targeted platform that lets them develop and launch ad campaigns on Search

Engine and its Display Network. It decides what advertisements are to be displayed on the search engine webpage and partner websites.

- AdSense is the publisher-oriented platform that lets publishers make money by putting advertisements on their websites. These publisher websites form a part of the search engine Display Network.
- AdMob is the same as AdSense except it is for mobile applications.

The search engine has two types of customers. first customers are the users who search, and the second type of customers is the businesses that advertise. Pretty much all the customers that Search Engine has are anybody who is looking for some form of information and Search Engine's value proposition is to find information for people. That's why you go to Search Engines because you want to find out something.

You want to find out a website. You want to find - when somebody's open. You want to find an answer to a particular question. You want to find a particular piece of knowledge. That is what Search Engine provides as a value to its free users.

The businesses that advertise on it, there the value that the Search Engine provides to them is targeting. It can very precisely Target customers who will be interested in, what the businesses are selling. So, for example, if somebody is looking to buy a bicycle in a particular city and Advertiser in that city can get a purchase Impressions on that particular keyword. There is a very high chance of being able to convert the purchase Impressions into sell. The Advertiser then can sell the customer bicycle and the sale from that pays for the advertising that it is paid for on Search Engine.

However, for all this system to work, I think an awful lot of people will miss to understand one thing; when they think about Search Engine's business model. If Search Engine has an awful lot of Partners and these are websites. Most websites in the world allow Search Engines to go through their website see what's on the website and Search Engine then use that information to create its index list of all the sites and all the information on those sites. If people didn't let Search Engine do that, if people did not let Search Engine see what information they have, it can find for free; Then Search Engine would not have a business model. Traditionally this information has been incredibly difficult to obtain.

If you think back to the early critics and guides, Critics had to go to each restaurant, in turn, to find out where it was, what sort of food, what quality of food that they serve. Search Engine can do this all automatically.

What relationships does Search Engine have with its users and advertisers? It has minimal Relationship. Almost no human contacts every search by a user. They type into a search bar also they gave a Voice command on Search Engine assistant. There is no human interaction at all or entirely mediated by computers. It is the same for the advertisers who use one of the advertising programs. They put the details of the advertising campaign and there is no

Design your business model

direct involvement of a human right to the front. Even the customer service of Search Engine is pretty much user-generated question-and-answer Pages FAQ Pages. It is very difficult to ever speak to a real-life person who works for a Search Engine.

When we come to the Channels, it's important to recognize that Search Engine has a website. Search Engine then makes its money by selling advertising. Users get to use Search Engine for free, however users do pay for the loss of privacy and giving away all the personal information for free to allow Search Engine to target adverts for the advertisers far more effectively. So that's how Search Engine makes its money. How? what are the resources? How does it build the infrastructure to do that? Well, it starts over here with the websites and basically what it does, is the index creation. It's continually updated index of all the information on all the websites in the world is a key resource for online search engine.

It's going everywhere on the web It read everything and it structure all that information into a massive index like what you get at the back of a book. Now if you have to go through that manually that will be incredibly time-consuming. But Search Engine does that itself in a few seconds and to do that the second key resource is the algorithms that allow Search Engine to analyze this vast amount of information and select the most relevant information that the user is searching for. To provide the algorithms to keep all this going, it basically needs computing power. You can treat this in several ways. It's

Search Engine's private VPN. Its undersea submarine cables and huge data centers all over the place. It has army of software Engineers, data scientists, etc. Those are the three key resources that Search Engine uses.

Basically, what they do is, they do Software engineering to make all this far more effective and optimize it. It uses data analytics to understand exactly, what is happening? Possibly you can also say that it buys other companies' other sources of information, which is a root-finding traffic optimization consumer product and that tells it where people are, where they're going, what they're doing. When you link that up with Search Engine Maps, it knows who you are where you've gone to, how you got there where you're going next time. This unparalleled amount of information comes into the team and it is live data that they use to improve the targeting in order to sell more to business advertisers and us to make more money.

Obviously, the Resources over here is the index, the algorithms and the computing power. These resources do cost, But It cost a lot less than the revenue that it brings in. So, this is people's costs. Plus, infrastructure and that, in essence, is the Search Engine, business model.

Business model in nutshell

(Online Search Engine)

Key Activities	Value Proposition	Customer Segment
• Maintenance of huge IT infrastructure • R&D and building new product • Develop existing products	• Free web searching • Fast and most relevant search results • Targeted advertisement • Display advertising management • Map, drive and other useful tools	• Internet users • Developers & Mobile owners • Advertisers
Key Resources • Datacenter • Newly and developed brands • Internet protocol		**Customer relationship** • Test Automation • Dedicated sales for large account
Key Partners • Distribution partners • Manufacturer for its designed devices		**Delivery Channels** • Global Sales force • Support team

Cost Structure	Revenue Stream
• Data center operation • R&D cost • Traffic acquisition cost	• Revenue from advertisers • Revenue from sales of own designed equipment (mobile and other)

Design your business model

CHAPTER 5

THE BUSINESS MODEL OF AN ONLINE RETAILER (E-COMMERCE)

The company is shipping 1.6 million packages per day! That's an unbelievable 608 million packages per year.

Who is the customer of e-commerce business? It's the mass market. Now people are quite busy with their job, hobby, relationships they don't want to go to the shop to buy a product. It's easier for them to visit an e-commerce website and order the product online. This market is huge consist of millions of people. It's especially useful for old people and the people having small children, for whom it's difficult to get to the shop.

The other benefit is product availability. If you visit a shopping store it may be quite large but online there is virtually no limit, you can put all the products available in all the stores through the world at just one place and you can use different filters to find out the best product you are looking for within minutes. It's all automated without any human interface while buying your product online.

When someone buy online and money transaction is made, the E-commerce platform charge commission to the seller.

Key resources are automation/software engineers and its warehouses' people who stores sellers' items in its warehouse.

Activities: Merchandise, Platform design, and optimization to look competitive and updated. Logistic and delivery services mostly provided by the third party, but e-commerce must align with them.

They also benefit from the economy of scales. Since they are selling in big amount

Let us assume the name of an e-commerce company is 'ABC'. Online retailer ABC operates a business model with many moving parts. The company sells some of its goods directly. A percentage of products are offered to buyers through ABC's online storefront with a small markup, and inventory is kept in the company's large network of warehouses. Most consumers visit the company's website assuming its products are cheaper and readily available for purchase and shipping.

In addition to direct sales, ABC provides a platform for other retailers to sell products to buyers. Products sold through ABC's partner retailers are often fewer common items or those with a higher purchase price, allowing ABC to avoid holding slow-moving inventory that could dilute profit. While ABC does not assess a fee for its retailer partners to list items for sale, the company does retain a portion of the sales price as commission.

ABC also maintains a subscription-based business model through its ABC Prime service, as well as a small electronics product line. Under a Prime account, customers pay an annual fee to secure free two-day or same-day shipping on eligible items and have access to streaming media, such as digital music or movies. ABC also generates revenue from selling its e-reader, e-book and mobile application.

Key Partners

Makers, outsider dealers, distributers and advanced substance makers are for the most part enter accomplices in ABC's operations.

Producers of the physical merchandise that are loaded in ABC's stockrooms are the conspicuous key accomplices. Notwithstanding, not every single physical item sold on ABC is put away in their distribution centers, and a generous level of income originates from outsider vendors who ABC permits to work on their online stage.

The general population who claim the protected innovation that ABC offers using the Kindle biological system and gushing stages are additionally key accomplices.

Key Activities

- Merchandising of its digital and physical goods.
- Development, design, and optimization of its Platform (website or apps).
- Manage supply chain and logistics
- Build and maintain a partnership with its supplier and sellers
- Support the production of movies or show on its online video platform
- Acquire new ventures to support its ecosystem

Key Resources

ABC possesses various physical assets, for example, distribution centers, and film studios, yet ABC's mechanical foundation is additionally a key asset. Notwithstanding owning numerous computerized content gushing stages, they are likewise the world's biggest supplier of cloud framework administrations through their auxiliary, ABC Web Services.

ABC's refined mechanical framework is a significant key asset that is fundamental for the everyday working of its business. For instance, ABC works a portion of the biggest databases on the planet, which they use to, in addition to other things, keep records on clients' utilization propensities with a specific end goal to participate in more effective marketing. In the period of "huge information", this is not a resource for being thought little of.

Client Segments

ABC claims to a mass market. Instead of focusing on socioeconomics, ABC's openness and a sheer assortment of physical and advanced items imply that anybody with a web association is a potential client. Regardless of whether it's physical merchandise or advanced media they are after, ABC has something to offer generally purchasers.

ABC additionally has a faithful center client section, apparently including a huge number of individuals all around, as its ABC Prime endorsers, who pay a yearly membership expense with the expectation of complimentary express postage and different advantages.

Channels

ABC's biggest channel is its site ABC.com. It likewise keeps up several distinct renditions of its site for clients from different nations crosswise over five landmasses. Items are additionally bought through the ABC advanced cell application, which works as an undeniably critical deals channel.

Some outsider gadgets stores stock ABC's Kindle scope of buyer hardware, giving an extra channel.

Client Relationships

Making internet shopping and the buy of computerized content simpler for customers has for some time been a concentration of ABC. Along these lines, ABC appreciates long haul associations with a huge number of customers overall who continue coming back to ABC consistently to purchase more items. They appreciate an especially cozy association with their ABC Prime supporters, who, having paid their yearly membership charge, is probably going to reliably utilize ABC as their first port of call for web-based shopping.

ABC.com offers a high level of client intuitiveness. Customers may survey buys and put remarks on each page. Along these lines, ABC is in some cases alluded to as the world's biggest retailer, as well as the biggest online group.

ABC puts vigorously on client benefit. To guarantee more elevated amounts of consumer loyalty, they offer 24-hour client benefits using email, telephone or web-visit, and also giving help discussions where clients may look for exhortation from the group.

Scalable

The business model of ABC is not very capital or human-intensive. This makes it scalable. ABC can easily enter another country and start selling products. Very little groundwork has to be done. This is the reason that ABC is going to be a multinational very soon. This asset-light business model is also preferred by investors who have pumped in billions of dollars for ABC to beat its competition with its deep pockets.

Competition

ABC faces a wide variety of competition from different types of companies. There are brick and mortar stores. Then there are other e-commerce sites and also video streaming sites like Netflix. However, none of these competitors seem to be formidable. ABC is the aggressor is almost all lines of business and is snatching business away from others rather than defending its turf.

Technology

ABC has always been at the center of several technological advancements since its inception in They have pioneered a new technology called contactless stores. The unique selling point of these stores is that there are no humans involved. ABC has achieved such high levels of automation, that they can run an entire departmental store without having any employees! It is technological advancements like these that will allow ABC to reach its ambitious revenue targets. Although at first, the revenue targets seem ludicrous, ABC seems to have a plan!

To sum it up, ABC has a unique business model. The hybrid tech cum retail model was pioneered by ABC. Ever since it has not let go of the first-mover advantage. Even today, this business pays no dividends and reinvests all the extra profits back into the operations signaling that ABC is still not a mature company and that it still preparing to grow rapidly.

Value Proposition

The value proposition provided by ABC is simple. They offer the most convenience, widest range of products and the lowest prices. Their prices are so low that they have displaced traditional shopping center leaders is low price category! The amazing part about ABC is that it provides goods and services at extremely low cost without compromising on quality by any means. ABC makes the lowest prices possible by leveraging technology. Firstly, it has leveraged technology in such a way that it does not have to stock inventory of any kind. While other stores are reeling under the massive cost burdens of stocking inventory, ABC can afford to undercut the competition on this.

It is a mix of a retail company as well as a technology company. Unlike, retail companies, ABC seldom hires stock clerks and floor managers. Their employees have high technological skills like data mining, programming etc.

Cost Structure

ABC's primary online retail exercises are taken a toll driven, implying that they work on a model whereby the economy of scale is imperative. Warehousing and circulation contain ABC's most noteworthy cost drivers as the organization works countless distribution centers internationally. ABC is chipping away at driving these expenses around computerizing stockroom preparing and conveyance where conceivable. Other critical cost drivers incorporate the running of many programming advancement focuses and client benefit bases on the world.

Another key cost is the underlying expense of acquiring the merchandise they offer, nonetheless, they can remain aggressive in this field by economies of scale.

ABC's protected innovation resources are esteem driven, with the encouraging environment and ABC's different gushing administrations working on the standard of making esteem as opposed to limiting expenses.

Revenue Model

ABC has a diverse revenue model.

- The primary source of revenue for ABC is the commissions that it obtains by making the buyers and sellers meet. ABC doesn't sell a lot of stuff on its own. It just provides a marketplace guaranteeing a standardized experience for both the buyers as well as the sellers.
- ABC also derives a huge chunk of its revenues from affiliate programs. ABC provides affiliates with stores within their sites. It then charges a larger commission on their sales.
- ABC also sells advertising space on its website. The ABC site is one of the most visited pages in any region. Hence, sellers can expect to boost sales by advertising on it. This is a minuscule portion of the

Design your business model

revenue that is generated by this company but is nonetheless significant.

- ABC also makes a huge chunk of money from the Kindle marketplace. ABC has developed and sold a device called Kindle. It can be used to read books in an electronic format. Thanks to this device, ABC has a 75% market share in the eBook market. Also, this market is highly profitable for ABC. Books sold by this model do not have to be published or transported. ABC, therefore, pockets the share of the publisher as well as the logistics firm. ABC gets close to 70% of the revenue generated by selling eBooks on Kindle.

- ABC has also developed subscription-based business models via its ABC Prime service. Using fixed subscription user get two benefits. Firstly, users can stream movies and video content via the internet. Secondly, ABC Prime members are entitled to lightning-fast delivery of the products purchased from ABC.

The revenue model of ABC is dynamic. It has been repeatedly venturing into newer regions. Also, technology is the backbone of the newer sources of revenue which many retailers had not thought about earlier.

Business model in nutshell

(Online Retailer (e-commerce))

Key Activities	Value Proposition	Customer Segment
• Merchandising, supply chain & logistic • Platform development & maintenance • Transfer of funds	• Convenience • A lot of options/variety • Low price compared to shops • Fast delivery • Warranty & easy return	• Internet & Mobile users • Buyers
Key Resources • Technology infrastructure • Online Platform & Network		**Customer relationship** • Customer support services • Review and comment • Social media & offers
Key Partners • Logistic • Sellers • Publishers		**Delivery Channels** • Mobile apps & website • Third party logistic

Cost Structure	Revenue Stream
• Operations of certain merchandise centers • Platform development, maintenance & R&D • Customer support centers	• Commission on transaction • E-commerce

CHAPTER 6

THE BUSINESS MODEL OF AN ONLINE PAYMENT/WALLET BUSINESS

The company has more than 450 million registered users. The average number of daily transactions is 5 million.

Let us assume XYZ is the name of an online payment/wallet business. XYZ is India's one of the largest mobile payments, e-wallet, and commerce platforms. Though started as a recharge platform, XYZ has subsequently changed its business model to a marketplace and a virtual bank model. It is also one of the pioneers of the cashback business model.

Design your business model

The company has changed itself into one of the Indian big companies dealing in mobile payments, banking services, marketplace, gold, recharge and bill payments, etc. It serves hundreds of million registered users.

Key Resources

The key resources that XYZ has are its Reserve Bank of India license and the design/software culture around designing applications that are easy for hundreds of millions of poorly educated Indians to use.

The RBI license is critical. This is an unusual banking license in India and seems to be specific to XYZ. It has allowed it to bypass substantial levels of regulations and acts as a barrier to entry for other competitors looking to imitate it.

Key Activities

XYZ, being a technology platform, risks dangers such as security and fraud which is why it must take effective measures in protecting its consumer's money by enhancing its security.

It is also making new changes within its platform to attract new users and gain access to their digital wallets.

Key Partners

XYZ partners with the banks that provide it with payment getaways into the banking system as well as escrow services.

Design your business model

It collaborates with a myriad of organizations that gather bills and payments from its consumers for its services.

Customers

XYZ serves Indian consumers and specifically Indian consumers who use mobile phones. Why is this important? Vast areas of India are underbanked and have a cash economy. In this case, India is like Kenya where M-Pesa evolved to solve a similar problem.

The pain that many people felt was that moving online and digital provided them with many opportunities, including the use of their mobile phones. However, for young people, it was difficult to open a bank account and pay for the services with a credit or debit card.

Similarly paying for phone data at a shop or street stall was time-consuming and poor customer experience. Neither allowed easy online payments. Much of this was due to the license raj, a cumbersome system of centralized control and bureaucracy that stifles innovation in many sectors

Customer Relationships

XYZ does not do customer relations with its users or the interface is almost negligible. It has no telephone or publicly available email or chat functionality. This is common to other e-commerce sites which focus on driving down their cost base.

Channel

XYZ uses many channels to attract customers. Apart from its website which drives clicks, it has formed partnerships with many client and vendor sites that sponsor its enterprise.

Demonetization in India allowed the company to prosper significantly and reach new customers as well. Offline marketing is also a part of their customer acquisition process.

Value Proposition

XYZ's initial value proposition solved this problem of under-banking and difficulty in recharging by providing a platform that was incredibly easy to use to top up mobile phone credit. This focus on usability meant that XYZ became more popular than the websites of mobile operators for phone recharging.

This is an important point. The core value that XYZ offered here was not that you could top up or recharge. Rather it was that it was so easy to do. It de-fractionalized a cumbersome process.

The second part of the value proposition was then to turn this into a parallel banking system. There is no good Western equivalent. PayPal offers similar services but 99% of its users have a bank account. 10 years back, most Indians did not.

By making it easy to move money between friends and families, customers and suppliers were then able to provide a valuable service. Because it was mobile-based it do not compete with the old money transaction systems that tie banks. This eWallet is now at the heart of XYZ's business model. "You can pay for anything easily"

This comes with huge network effects. XYZ becomes far more valuable to its users as more people use it.

Once some e-commerce puts some investment the focus has shifted to moving from being an online payment services provider which is offered on multiple sites. XYZ is increasingly trying to move vendors onto its site creating a closed ecosystem. This is like the evolution of WeChat from a messaging system to an integrated marketplace. This is a defensive move as economies of scale seem to be the optimum model in eCommerce sites as Alibaba and Amazon demonstrate,

XYZ has faced an educational problem in persuading customers to try its novel electronic payments system. As a result, it has had to use a variety of channels. The most important of these were the partnerships that it established originally with mobile providers. In their billing, they offered XYZ as an option and this allowed XYZ to reach millions of customers at low cost quickly. Each additional payment customer added large numbers of users and increased awareness of non-converted Indians of the ubiquity of the platform.

Design your business model

XYZ invested heavily in cricket and TV advertising. This created awareness and provided credibility to the brand as it drew on the status of existing advertisers of major sporting events.

Finally, demonetization in India in 2016 increased XYZ' user base by over 20 million in less than a month as people were forced away from cash banking and chose to use XYZ rather than use retail banks

Cost Structure

XYZ serves many customers that the reason why it is so cost-driven. Most of its expenses are related to its platform and customer acquisition. It's a common expense shared by many businesses across the world where customer acquisition cost is substantial. The money used in this process is higher than the revenue it makes in its initial purchases.

Most of its budget is invested in ramping up of its security and avoid the risk of fraud especially when it has to handle over 65 million customers in its platform. It includes a system that enables customers to prevent any money laundering risk.

Revenue Stream

The XYZ Revenue Models come in two forms.

- XYZ makes commissions from customer transactions through its usage of its platform.
- Escrow Accounts – escrow accounts from where it generates its revenue. Owing to the absence of its underlying capital, it offers customers no interest.

XYZ Revenue Model can be divided into the following categories.

- Marketplace (Web e-commerce, App commerce, etc.)
- Recharge Services
- Bill Payments
- Payment Solutions
- XYZ Wallet
- Digital Gold
- XYZ Bank

The Recharge Business

This business is what they started with. They create one of the earliest platforms for phone recharges, which were much simpler than the offline mode of it. For recharges, XYZ earns a commission of 2 to 3% per recharge. The recharge market is worth millions of dollars. And XYZ controls about 30% of this market. This will hand them a handsome sum of money. This business will get stagnant after a while when penetration has reached far enough, and the subscriber base doesn't grow. It's constant money and more importantly, it's traffic to the website. This business is what has fueled their growth and right now it provides traffic and a database to upsell their next business.

The E-commerce Business

Everybody is seeing the value of the e-commerce marketplace business. It's a great way to earn a profit on the items sold and the online channel makes it much more potent than the online channel. XYZ has done just that. They got into the e-commerce business and promoted their e-commerce platform to their existing users. They've recently tied up with over 1,000 brands to set up mini shops within XYZ to truly create a marketplace. This would be run exactly like an offline channel, to explain it further it would be run like a mall. The brands would control their brands' experience and XYZ would earn a percentage of every sale.

The Wallet Business

The wallet business of the number one competitor that grew into a $60 Billion business could be replicated in India by XYZ. They got the license for a pre-paid wallet from the Government of India and are hoping to tap into the banked and the unbanked. This wallet would be the front for all payments where you could buy a movie ticket to paying the milkman with this wallet. It would be a one-touch payment for every sale, which makes it extremely hassle-free. Having a service-connected directly with a wallet is what XYZ believes will be a differentiator in e-commerce as well. They make commissions from the retailers for every transaction that is made through the wallet.

Business model in nutshell

(Online payment/wallet business)

Key Activities	Value Proposition	Customer Segment
• Fraud protection • Data security, Platform maintenance • Transfer of funds	• Easy way to Recharging and bill payment • E-wallet • E-commerce • Cheaper than other transaction mode(By giving cashback)	• Mobile users • E wallet users
Key Resources • RBI license • Technology • Platform & Network		**Customer relationship** • Customer support services • App & website • Social media & offers
Key Partners • Movie theater, travel sites & Hotels • Shopping centers and Banks • Investors		**Delivery Channels** • Mobile apps & website • Client and vendor sites
Cost Structure		**Revenue Stream**
• Customer acquisition cost • Platform development, maintenance & R&D • Customer support		• Commission on transaction • E-commerce

Design your business model

CHAPTER 7

THE BUSINESS MODEL OF 24/7 ON-DEMAND, APP-BASED TAXI-SERVICE

This company provided 583,000 rides every hour or an average of 14 million rides a day

It is a Business Model of a taxi aggregator which has brought a revolution in the taxi industry all across the world. The business model has made it possible for people to simply tap their smartphone and have a cab arrive at their door step in the minimum possible time. This business is a smartphone app which provides on-demand service to users. It connects willing passengers to taxicab drivers. Taxi drivers use their cars when providing taxi service and This business gets almost 20%-25% of the fare. The total process is very simple, registered users ask for a taxi using the This business app, a driver then dispatched to the passenger's location by the app and assist the passengers to reach his destination. The passenger's credit card is used as the sole payment method.

4 step model about how This business works

- *Step 1 (Request a cab):* The first step in the business model is about creating a demand. People have a smartphone app that lets them request a cab instantly or schedule it for some time later.
- *Step 2 (Matching):* As soon as the request is made, a notification about your details are sent to the nearest driver. The cab driver has the option to accept or reject the ride. In case he rejects, notification is sent to another driver nearby that area.
- *Step 3 (Ride):* Customer can track the cab when it is arriving, and the ETA is also shown to the customer. The meter starts as soon as the customer sits in the cab and provide OTP, which can be tracked through the customer side app as well. Drivers make sure that the ride is comfortable for the passenger and they can get good feedback from customers.
- *Step 4 (Payment & Rating):* Once the ride is over, the customer gets an option to rate the driver. Rating system is an important part of the business model as it lets a person know about the driver before booking a ride and helps him trust the driver

Key activities

Positive indirect network effects are the key ingredient of platform businesses to achieving competitive advantage. The key activities should revolve around enhancing positive indirect network effects and reducing negative ones.

- Remove friction from all interactions
- Appropriately connect driver and customer side to reduce idle times for drivers and waiting times for customers
- Reduce negative externalizes, e.g. bad behaviors on both sides.
- Grow the platform by getting more users joining it.
- Keep participants engaged and stimulate ongoing participation
- Continue improving the value proposition, e.g. cheaper rides for regular commuters through common POOL service
- Look out for complementary value propositions (e.g. car financing, new customer segments, etc.)
- Deliver on the customer proposition
- Expand to more cities
- Analyze the data to fine-tune everything
- Enhance technological lead and intellectual property to steepen barriers of entry

Key Partners

- The drivers are on the supply side of this business and they can join or leave at a moment's notice. It is essential to have enough of them to be able to provide the customer proposition (timely pick-up at low cost). They bring their cars into the value proposition for this business and do not have to outlay any capital costs. Without a critical mass of drivers, the crucial indirect network effects do not kick-in which is why This business accelerates supply when they enter a new city.
- This business has its technology staff which should be listed under key (human) resources. Cloud providers (and many other standard technology and infrastructure providers) are not key partners if what they provide is easy to switch. Partners that offer leading-edge technology, proprietary (and ideally exclusively provided) functionality would be in the key partner category.
- Investors/venture capitalists bring the initial rounds of funding to the table. The funding helps to develop the functionality, apps, algorithms, driver-less cars but is also used for customers' acquisition costs and other expenditures.

Key resources

The master resource of your platform is its network effects. It is the resource that needs to be built and nurtured. The data, the algorithms and the capability to analyze and gain

Design your business model

insights are essential. The latter also grows with the size of the network.

- Network effect of the participants (drivers and riders)
- Captured data, algorithms
- Analytic capabilities
- Skilled engineering & other staff
- Platform architecture
- Venture capital to keep the business growing
- Brand name & assets
- The rider and the driver app and other products

Customer relationships

This business needs to consider four elements to manage their customer relationships. Their relationships to (1) the customers(=riders), (2) the drivers, (3) the broader public and (4) regulators.

Relevant for drivers & customers

- Manage any safety risks
- Manage bad behaviors (on both sides drivers and passenger) and improve rules continuously
- Deal with customer issues in an appropriate manner and timeliness.
- Transparent pricing, e.g. criticism on surge pricing by riders and decreasing hourly income by drivers
- Transparency around privacy

- Portray the desired company image through social and other media

Especially for the drivers

Customer relationships to the supply side (the driver) will be mainly defined by what the platform does for them, examples are:

- Acceptable hourly wages
- Acceptable working conditions and hours
- Manage issues (accidents, damages or issues affecting earnings)
- Support in the on-boarding process where required
- Fair allocation of rides (algorithmic ride allocation avoids favoritism issues with the traditional dispatcher)
- This business is working on a trial program for enabling affordable private insurance (medical, injury, disability, life)
- This business's perspective: avoid groups of drivers to reduce risk of unionization

The public

This business is working on portraying a positive image by claiming positive contributions to the communities:

- Pointing out a positive impact on the environment, e.g. reducing emissions through common POOL service.

- Making communities safer, e.g. through reducing driving under the influence
- How This business puts pressure on regulators through their communication campaigns.
- Manage the platform's image across the media and other relevant channels (workplace culture, leadership shadows)

Customer Segments

Being a one-stop solution for every need, this business's most targeted audience is full-time job seekers as they are amongst the maximum ratio to use This business Cabs. Whereas college-goers find it useful in case of unavailability of the other means of public transport. For tourists, it's bliss, this business has made their hustle bustle from one place to another enormously smoother. It has made various activities of users like attending an important meeting, parties or events when running out of time or escaping on a rainy day much comfortable.

This business has such a vast customer segment that it has got something on offer for everyone. This business Taxis to This business Black and from This business X to This business SUV, the company has got a vast range for its customers to make a choice.

In short, Following constitute the customer base for this business

- Do not own a car.

Design your business model

- Do not want to drive themselves to a party or function.
- Like to travel in style and want to be treated like a VIP.
- Want a cost-efficient cab at their doorstep.

Channels

Channels for the initial awareness and customer acquisition:

- Campaigns: free vouchers when This business enters a new city (e.g. handed out at public transport stations)
- Free media coverage based on the novelty factor (new joiners have often soared even after extensive negative coverage)
- Word of mouth
- Social media, people sharing
- Digital ad campaigns
- App stores of iOS, Android, window, etc. – through high ratings, ads and being featured

Value Propositions

Customers:

- No long waiting time for a taxi.
- Free rides on certain occasions and discounts from time to time.
- Cheaper than the normal taxi fares.
- This business provides the same as a personal driver. It lets customers travel in style.

Design your business model

- Fixed prices for common places like Airport, bus station etc.
- There's no refusal, unless in extreme cases when the driver can't make it to the location within time, or when there are no cars available.
- The system of reviewing and rating a ride, as well as complaining in case of any mishap is something taxis are lacing in.
- The time constraint within which the cab is going to show up is always mentioned before a ride.
- The driver can be contacted and all his details, including contact number and car details, are shown to the client before the ride commences.
- The route could be altered as per the flexibility of the client
- The rates are reduced considerably in the case of common Pool – a ride-sharing service.
- There are a variety of car types to choose from depending on the number of people and also on the standard of the ride.
- They have even started accepting cash payments which are paid directly to the driver
- A user can tap his smartphone and call a cab at his location in just 3 clicks on phone screen.
- If a driver accepts the ride, driver details are sent to the customer along with ETA.
- The customer can track the taxi as it arrives at his location.
- The business model had a rating system in place for drivers, where a customer can rate the driver after his ride.

Drivers:

- An additional source of income.
- Flexible working schedules. They can work part-time or simply whenever they like.
- Easy payment procedure.
- Those who love to drive can earn money, whenever they like, while pursuing their hobby.
- This business pays drivers to be online, even if they don't get any request.
- They have the option to accept or reject a ride.

Cost structure

For many online platforms, the biggest cost element is customer acquisition costs (CAC). This is not different for this business and its competitors. The weapon of choice was customer acquisition "subsidies" (on both sides the drivers and the passengers).

The cost element is:

- Cost of customer acquisition 'CAC': discount vouchers, subsidies on memberships, digital advertising, etc.
- The weighted average cost of capital, WACC : on business
- Development of new features, ongoing fine-tuning of algorithms, etc.
- Common Pool driver costs

- Legal cases and settlement costs
- Lobbying, regulatory compliance
- Transaction fees (credit card charges)
- Salaries for staff and share-based compensation
- Expansion to more cities and countries
- Infrastructure costs, computing power, bandwidth
- Customer support
- Insurance costs
- Research & development, e.g. autonomous vehicles
- Expansion to adjacent niches (This business EATS, etc.) initially cash negative

They don't put driver wages as a cost element. But This business revenues only include what This business takes as transaction revenues, i.e. 20%-30% of the fare. Thus, there are no driver costs or payouts as such. "Revenue includes only the portion this business takes from fares. Only exception is the case of its carpooling service; the company counts the entire amount of a common Pool fare as revenue." This way of accounting also aligns with how other platform businesses account. The reason for accounting common Pool rides differently is likely because This business's share on these rides may exceed the driver's share.

Revenue Stream

This business collaborates with vehicle owners and drivers and together they set up a minimum charge at which the partners will operate. This business supplies them riders through online bookings from one single application and charges some amount of commission from them. The commission charged by the company ranges from 20% – 25% of the total amount charged from the customer.

Price Calculation

This business sets the price of a ride as per kilometer charges and the time spent.

Dynamic Pricing

- On bad weather days, hours of traffic congestion and public holidays, when the demand for cab rides is higher than their availability, this business clients must deal with price surges. The company is transparent about this dynamic pricing strategy and informs the riders beforehand if there's an increase in the price of the cab. Surging in cab fares according to situation is an important aspect of their business model. Whenever the demand increases, prices automatically increased.
The new price depends on the number of available drivers and the number of requests made by people who want to travel in a particular area.

Learning from This Business Model:

- In most cases, owning inventory is a liability and the This business model of business is such a relief in this regard. Go for less ownership model. This business does not own any cab but still provides over a million rides a day through its partner network.

- Choose an industry. Find the most common problem it has. Find a solution and disrupt the existing model with the help of technological infrastructure. That is what This business did in the cab industry. Use the internet for new business and growth of the present business.
- Treat your initial users as kings. They are important for the growth of your business.
- Deliver a swift and efficient service and charge at least a 15% commission for any transaction.
- Expand step by step. Do not add everything to your business model in the first go. This business started with cabs but now even has boats, helicopters, bikes, and other means.
- Opportunity won't come to you. You must look for them. This business created an opportunity by offering discounted rides for events/party venues and hence got its first customers.
- Treat your workforce as an important part of your business. This business calls its driver as partners and gives them a decent 80% of the total fare.
- Take full advantage of the free market economy.
- There is no such thing as bad publicity, this business's frequent visits to the courts, actually helped the company to grow. But understand the difference, bad publicity, and being bad are two different things.

- This business is a highly profitable company and revenues are doubling every 6 months. It has far better expansion opportunities than most of the Fortune 500 companies.

Business model in nutshell

(24/7 on-demand, app-based taxi service)

Key Activities	Value Proposition	Customer Segment
• Sales promotion & marketing • Platform development & maintenance • Communication with drivers & users	**For User** • Lower price than available taxi services • Safety, security & easy transaction **For Driver** • Ease in accessing more passengers • Freedom to choose working hours • Opportunity to earn	• Drivers • Users • Developer
Key Resources • Brand Image • Software & Technology • Platform & Network		**Customer relationship** • Users & drivers are core of system • Govt regulators • General public
Key Partners • Drivers • Investors • Lobbyist		**Delivery Channels** • Mobile apps & website • Word of mouth • Social media & offers
Cost Structure • Customer acquisition cost • Platform development, maintenance & R&D • Insurance, legal & settlement cost • Customer support		**Revenue Stream** • Ride transaction fee • License fee

Design your business model

CHAPTER 8

THE BUSINESS MODEL OF A 'DIGITAL SOCIAL MEDIA NETWORK' COMPANY

With 2.41 billion monthly active users this company is the biggest social network worldwide.

Let us assume, 'X' is the name of a digital social media network. Company 'X' is one of the most loved social media network website & apps. The estimated number of daily active users for it is over a billion. Company 'X' has built arguably the best business model in the world, achieving the trifecta of high scale *and* high growth *and* high-profit margins unmatched by any high-tech company.

Teenagers in today's day and age have shifted too much simpler social media apps but people at Company 'X' have

Design your business model

implemented a simple strategy: if you can't beat them, acquire them. Having already made many acquisitions so far.

Company 'X' was launched way before the apps came into the picture. Targeting the college/university going students, Company 'X' was an idea to connect students from all over the country. Sighting the popularity of Company 'X', they launched a sign-up form right at the homepage of the website. All you need is a valid email ID. Based on the information you provide to Company 'X' like your workplace, university or interests, Company 'X' will show you people that you may know so that you can add them to your friends' list. There is a search bar where you can find your friends, relatives, neighbors, colleagues and interests like pages or groups. You can also start a group, or a page related to your business or a common interest and invite people to like & follow it.

How it works

The Wall: The center of all is the "wall". It is like a graffiti wall where people write stuff and you read to it when you pass from there. The wall is a timeline which used to show posts in chronological order earlier but now shows posts based on relevance and popularity. You or your friends can upload a picture or a video, write something or mark an activity like travel or have a meal on the wall. You can also tag the places you are at using the online map empowered location services.

Design your business model

Messenger: Company 'X' website had an integrated tab for chatting where you could send messages to anyone. You could chat if that person was online at the same time. Now, Company 'X' has a separate affiliated app for instant messaging called the Company 'X' Messenger.

Notification: Company 'X' would notify you every time there is an activity concerning you. It could be someone commenting on a post you liked or someone liking your picture/video/post, or it could be a notification to tell you that someone has tagged you in a post. These are push notifications for apps. In the last few years, Company 'X' sends notifications which are suggestions which may not concern you.

Other features: There are dozens of other exciting features on Company 'X'. With time, Company 'X' has made some great innovations and introduced features that have changed the way people socialize on the internet. You can create Company 'X' events & invite people to that. These events provide information about real events. There is a marketplace where you can buy stuff. It is not a conventional e-commerce platform, but a list of things available near your location from local stores, mainly restaurants. You can create a live event as well that will stream you live from your mobile or laptop front camera on the wall of your friends. The list of exciting Company 'X' features is long. Recently, stories were launched on Company 'X' & other two giant apps owned by Company 'X' such as Instagram & WhatsApp. Stories are images or videos flashing across your screen in a presentable manner. You can tap on stories to jump to the next stories. These stories have a timeline of 24 hours and they auto disappear after 24 hours. Each year, Company 'X' comes up with innovative features and a change in the user interface that changes the users' experience.

Key Activities

Platform development & maintenance – Company 'X' is a platform that produces a myriad of activities. One of them being its web development alongside App Development and game development.

Data maintenance and security – Invest in user data security and privacy.

Establish partnership & develop new offer – It offers other activities like projects, marketing, software development and other forms of innovation which it has been duly credited for.

Strategic acquisition – such as Image sharing apps, instant massaging apps, and other social media-related apps.

Maintain government regulations – complying with laws in different countries is essential for Company 'X' operations.

Hire & retain talent

Sales, marketing and operations

Key Partners

Company 'XQ's platform continues to create new partners for it as it grows. Mobile operating system developers (iOS, Android), credit card companies, Mobile handset manufacturers, and browser developers have collaborated with Company 'X'.

Key Resources

Platform and Brand name – Company 'X' utilizes its platform as its primary resource to access more users and advertiser. The more users access and log in to its site the more subsidiaries it receives.

Network – Company 'XQ's network has provided limitless communication opportunities for its users despite their background.

Technology talent – Company 'X' takes immense pride in its technology and pool of talented employees. It was able to hire and retain. Thanks to its brand value.

Customers Segment

Users – Company 'XQ's customers mostly comprise of its users. Users who wish to communicate with different people and interact with those in the outside world. Company 'X' is now its marketplace where users can buy and sell a property like clothes and jewelry and even fundraise for their respective causes.

Advertisers and Marketers – Brands and advertisers also form a part of its customer base that earns revenue for the company by placing offers and promotional ads.

Developers – The site also has its App and Game development platform where users can play while the

Design your business model

game developers like Zynga and Company 'X' both benefits.

Customer Relationships

Self Service platform – Company 'XQ's network and site are user-friendly and easily accessible for its users. It assists new users through its instructions to form their accounts and identities. The users gradually get the hang of it and realize how easy it can be utilized.

Self-Taught Site – It is a self-learning site. You can expand your online visibility by finding more friends through your new profile owing to Company 'XQ's community-building applications.

Global Salesforce – Company 'X' has an extensive global sales organization that works directly with Advertising agencies and ad resellers. Sales work to attract, retain and support advertisers.

Channel

Internet – The first prerequisite is the Internet for its service; Company 'X' operates through the Internet via Laptops, Computers, Tablets or Smartphones.

Website & mobile apps– Then, it makes its usage of its website and mobile app to reach more users. Through its site, Company 'X' allows advertisers to market their products. Many public figures and celebrities have also contributed to its channeling efforts.

Third-party developer Tools and APIs – These are used by developers for channeling purposes as well. Other partnerships assist in these purposes in their distinct ways depending on the agreement.

Value proposition

Social media network

World's most favorite social media network, Company 'X' lets you connect with your friends, family, and others. It also launched its less data consumption version, Company 'X' Lite.

Global Connectivity – Company 'X' has made it its mission to spread a free medium of communication and connectivity with people across the world regardless of their nationality, religion, culture or background.

Sharing of ideas – It is a platform where different people can interact with each other and expose themselves to different cultures, experiences, and ideas.

Brand promotion – It is a platform where you can showcase your talents as well as play games whenever you want.

Easy Accessibility – There is no time limit where its network is concerned. Whatever you wish to search will be delivered in your domain.

Messenger

Company 'X'.com separated chat from its interface and launched Messenger as a mobile messaging app with which users can send private messages and stickers, chat with groups, and make free calls, even to people in other countries.

Company 'X' has also integrated payments in messenger for users residing in some countries

Workplace

Workplace by Company 'X' is an in-house social network for companies to connect with everyone in their company. A workplace profile will be different from that of a Company 'X' personal profile and companies will be charged to register for a Workplace Profile for their employees.

Marketplace

Company 'X' has taken a step forward with the introduction marketplace. The working model of Company 'X' Marketplace will be the same as that of other online marketplaces but with an integration of messenger. Hence making it a social marketplace. Payments will not be made on Company 'XQ's platform though.

Moments

A competitor to photo storage apps, which lets you sync your photos to the cloud. Not just it, it is cloud storage which will sync and form an album of all the photos you and your friends upload if they were taken on the same date & place and you were a part of it.

Image Sharing app

The second most loved social media network after Company 'X'. It is an image sharing network which lets you share moments with everyone you're connected to. Unlike Company 'X', Instagram has a follower network which lets you share your photos with your followers.

image stories have been introduced by Company 'X' to get an edge in its competition with other similar apps.

Visual filters app

it is a mobile application that provides users with visual filters and faces swipe technology which can be used while taking pictures.

Instant messaging client

World's leading instant messaging client. This messaging service is an end to end encrypted and fully digitized instant messaging service which uses the internet to send & receive messages and competes to the typical SMS services.

Virtual reality – with the acquisition of Oculus, Company 'X' is trying its hand in the field of virtual reality hardware.

Payment infrastructure – Users can purchase digital goods or applications from developers using Company 'X' payment services.

Cost Structure

It's the cost of infrastructure Company 'X' is built on. It includes expenses related to the delivery and distribution of products, its depreciation, and other costs. Costs such as-

facility and server equipment expense and depreciation, energy and bandwidth costs, support and maintenance costs

Research & Development

Company 'X' is the world's number one social media network. This doesn't mean that it has no competition and will remain at the top forever. Company 'X' and it's family companies have had loads of competitors in the market and have successfully been able to suppress them all due to an insane amount of research and development.

Hence, R&D is of utmost importance to Company 'X' to retain and to grow. Research and development have proved out to be a major expense item for Company 'X' that could continue to see a significant lift in the coming quarters. Company 'X' is always looking to enhance its user experience. R&D has a great role in it.

Design your business model

Marketing and sales cost

Company 'X' is one of the biggest brands. It's a costly affair to maintain it. Company 'XQ's marketing and sales cost include

- Expenses for better user interface and other services provided to users, marketers, and developers to attract and retain them.
- Amortization of intangible assets
- Payrolls and other benefit costs
- Other marketing and sales expenses incurred on people and products.

General and Administrative

This includes compensation to the employees of administrative departments and other legal and accounting expenses.

Revenue Sources

Company 'X' making huge revenue, approximately 89 percent of which came from digital advertisements. But unlike its rival, which allows advertisers to connect with consumers through keyword searches, Company 'X' generates revenue primarily from targeted advertising and user data.

Hold on a second, user data? That's right. It is alleged that Company 'X' has compromised user data, privacy, and security by granting multinational companies access to the personal information of its users. Some newspaper alleges that these social sites give several multinational companies the ability to access users' contact information, private messages, and friend lists. The companies include big names, which had access to users' private messages. Now, these social media say that the company had stopped selling access to user data years ago.

We don't want to go into the investigation, was it true or allegation. But one thing comes out for sure, these companies are somehow tracking the user behavior to tap on advertisement which can be a potential selling opportunity.

Making Money from Ads?

Ads are everywhere on Company 'X'. Some are sponsored ads & others are those ads that are based on your geographic & demographic data. For instance, if you have searched for some products on the search engine, you will likely see advertisements for similar products on your Company 'X' home page. The browser saves your searches as cookies & cache memory and shares it with many other apps who have the algorithm to quickly show you sponsored similar results on their pages. So next time if you search for something & Company 'X' tries to suggest something similar, don't freak out. So far, we could only see ads in public places such as our timeline & on either side of our timeline on the Company 'X' website. But Company 'X' is reportedly looking to pop up ads in open & closed groups as well. Groups that have higher frequency are very much likely to have ads in them shortly. For apps like cab booking or food delivery or photo sharing, there is very limited information available about users to the advertisers. So, they just risk advertising their products to them expecting them to like it. But with Company 'X', they know the likes, dislikes, political inclination, choices of food, views on cinema & also geographic locations of every user. This helps the companies hugely target their audiences. That's exactly the reason why some Company 'X' ads cost way more than television or radio commercials

If you want to build a community & bring the world closer that helps connect everyone in the world, then there are a lot of people who can't afford to pay. Therefore, with a lot of media, having an advertising-supported model is the only rational model that can support building this service.

Advertisers can use the wealth of personal data about users from Company 'XQ's product ecosystem for ads. For its part, one California-based company alleges that it makes the data anonymous and serves the information to advertisers in custom demographic buckets. Advertisers can further divide the bucket of information up into smaller parts based on their branding goals. They can serve up custom ads to Company 'X' users from specific income groups or regions, and target users based on other categories, such as sexual orientation, religion or political affiliation. Company 'X' has developed a broad variety of ad products for different stages of the branding lifecycle.

For example, its Company 'X' Dynamic Ads product enables advertisers to upload their entire product catalog and target customers at specific income levels.

Making Money from Video Content?

The company is preparing for the future by broadening its revenue canvas. It has emphasized videos and live broadcasts from its Live platform in its earnings calls in recent quarters. According to the company, the daily watch time for Company 'X' Live broadcasts has grown by more than four times in the past year. The social media giant has also inked deals with content creators to further promote the video.

Making Money from messenger service

Another emerging area of growth for Company 'X' is its messenger service, which has begun displaying ads. The service's direct chat feature, which enables customers to chat directly with advertising businesses, already saw more than a billion messages being exchanged between users in a quarter.

Company 'X' also has invested in emerging technology trends for future growth. Included among these use cases in virtual reality and bringing internet to parts of the world without connectivity. Again, these initiatives translate into future sources of revenue for Company 'X', as more internet connections translate to greater usage and revenue.

Making Money from User Data?

Design your business model

It's hard to be sure how much money Company 'X' makes from user data because targeted advertisements, by definition, show users relevant ads by using their data. Some analytics claim that Company 'X' had been making money from user data far more directly than imagined.

Audience Network

A new competitor to Google AdSense. Company 'X' already has millions of advertisers and now, according to its new strategy, it'll share them with some mobile applications and website developers. Audience Network is an advertising network powered by Company 'X' which appears on apps and mobile websites other than just Company 'X' family companies.

What they are paying for

While Company 'X' invites advertisers of all sizes, they're all after the same thing likes and shares.
The cost of ads may varies in ranges from 5 cents to 5 dollars per click. Cost goes up based on targeting and engagement.

Sidebar ads

The most common ads, appear on the side of the site. May Cost about $1-$5 with most types of targeting.

Sponsored stories

Design your business model

Status updates from businesses turned into ads. May cost around 50 cents per click since they get higher engagement (more likes and comments).

Promoted posts

Posts that are targeted to fans and 'friends & family' of fans: It may cost about $5 per every 1,000 people targeted.

Business model in nutshell

('Digital social media network' Company)

Key Activities	Value Proposition	Customer Segment
• Data security • Platform development & maintenance • Strategic acquisition & partnership	• Global Connectivity • Easy accessibility • Huge marketplace • Payment infrastructure • Sharing of ideas • Free of cost for users	• Users (almost everyone) • Advertisers and marketers • Developer
Key Resources • Software & Technology • Platform • Network		**Customer relationship** • Self taught Platform • Self service platform • Global salesforce
Key Partners • Third party • Content creator		**Delivery Channels** • Mobile apps • Internet • Website

Cost Structure	Revenue Stream
• Data protection • Platform development & maintenance • R&D • Customer service and marketing cost	• Advertisement revenue • Payment revenue

Design your business model

CHAPTER 9

THE BUSINESS MODEL OF 'ONLINE TRAVEL ACCOMODATION MARKETPLACE'

The company does not own any of the real estate properties, nor does it host events. Today, Company 'A' is present in more than 30,000 cities across 180+ countries. You can imagine the scale, Company 'A' sees more than 140000+ people staying at its homestays every day.

Let us assume 'A' is the name of an online travel accommodation marketplace. Company 'A' utilizes an

Aggregator Business Model. Company 'A' is an online marketplace connecting travelers with local hosts. The platform enables people to list their available space and earn extra income in the form of rent. On the other side, Company 'A' enables travelers to book unique homestays from local hosts, saving them money and giving them a chance to interact with locals. Catering to the on-demand travel industry, Company 'A' is present in the majority of countries across the world. The company does not own any of the real estate properties, nor does it host events;

Today, Company 'A' is present in more than 30,000 cities across 180+ countries. You can imagine the scale, Company 'A' sees more than 140000+ people staying at its homestays every day.

How Company 'A' works:

Hosts list out their property details on Company 'A' along with other factors like pricing, amenities provided, etc.

Company 'A' sends a professional photographer(if available) to the property location to take high-quality photographs.

Travelers search for a property in the city where they wish to stay and browse available options according to price, amenities, etc.

Booking is made through Company 'A' where traveler pays the amount mentioned by the host and some additional money as transaction charges.

Host approves the booking. Traveler stays there and finally, Company 'A' pays the amount to the host after deducting their commission.

The host and the traveler can rate each other and can write reviews based on the experience.

Key activities

The network effects are the moat (i.e. competitive advantage) of platform businesses. The key activities revolve around improving positive network effects and reducing negative ones.

Enhance positive network effects between the participants (hosts and guests), by enticing more users to join and participate

Reduce negative network effects, by making the individual host-guest transactions easier and transparent. Managing complaints swiftly and learning from them

Grow the platform by:

- Getting more participants to join,
- Entering new cities,
- Complementary offering that increases stickiness, such as events.

Keep participants engaged, e.g. high utilization of homes

Design your business model

Keep guests returning by providing great service to them for travel experiences in accommodation and events/experiences

Add new customer value propositions, e.g. event hosting:

- Creates complementary offerings to lodging,
- Adds new hosts and offer them income opportunities,
- Increases host and guest engagement

Deliver on the customer proposition

Analyze the data to fine-tune everything, example on improving the check-in process

Key partners

Key partners are not easily replaceable. They contribute significantly to the success of the company and influence its future trajectory.

Hosts are the supply side of the Company 'A' platform. They bring their homes/units to the table. Achieving a critical mass of supply and variety of choice is important for the customer value proposition. Company 'A' has two types of hosts:

Rental hosts offer houses, units/condos, rooms, and more exotic stays, such as castles, igloos and more.

Event hosts offers to guide on local experiences, food, art, fashion, nightlife, etc.

Investors/venture capitalists bring the initial rounds of funding to the table. The funding helps with developing the functionality, apps, algorithms, but also for acquiring customers. Investors bring down the (weighted) cost of capital (WACC). Funding rounds for Company 'A' are crucial to keep costs of capital low, to expand and run operations until the platform becomes profitable

Influencers are crucial for Company 'A' at all levels of government. The exception is to share rooms in the same apartment, where the landlord stays. Company 'A' has ramped up its lobbying effort at all levels. The aggregate success of their lobbyists can make a considerable difference to Company's trajectory.

Corporate travel planners: Company 'A' has opened a large source of new guests by expanding into the business travel world. Through their alliances with other online travel portals, Company 'A' inventory becomes available to corporate travel managers.

Corporate travel managers have some discretion as to which suppliers, including lodging providers, they enlist within their corporate travel policies. These corporate travel managers have the discretion to add thousands of potential guests. Early adopters are particularly valuable as they can set a precedent for peers to follow.

Other partners

Those where Company 'A' has several options with comparable offerings to choose from. This doesn't mean the service non-key partners are providing is unimportant:

Company 'A' hires freelancing professional streets/events/property photographers in some cities. The photos are very important. But there is sufficient supply of photographers. Even if all current photographers decided to jump ship, it would not affect Company's revenues and within a few weeks, they would fill the ranks back up.

Maps, payment platforms, cloud storage, identification platforms are important, but they are not proprietary any more in today's world.

Insurance companies, while very important and initially challenging to make a deal with, by now it's not a challenge any longer.

Cloud providers (and many other tech API providers) are not key partners if they provide easy-to-replace commodities (unlike a few years ago). Company 'A' has acquired several small tech companies that may end up becoming key resources if they contribute significantly to Company's growth.

Key resources

The key resources of this business are the network effects. Here it is between hosts and guests. Company 'A' is a great example of this. Company 'A' hosts are providing places to stay, events, recommendations what to do at the locations. Not every host does all and that is not required. On aggregate, the hosts make their destinations (and thus traveling as such) more attractive by indirectly collaborating. This is a great example that the total is larger than the sum of the individual parts.

The value propositions listed in the next section unfold their strength with the network's effects.

With this said, the key resources are:

- The network effects
- The homes listed & requested
- The events listed & requested
- User-generated content on the webpages
- Captured data
- The algorithms

Development, analytic capabilities, and engineers, data scientists

- The brand

Design your business model

- Access to venture capital to keep the business growing
- Skilled employees
- The app & webpages

The Problems and Solutions:

Trust Problem: The biggest problem faced by travelers or hosts using Company 'A' is the trust factor. After all, giving your space to a stranger as a host and living with strangers at their place as a traveler might not be easy. But the verification process is there for every host and traveler on its platform. Apart from the verification badge, Company 'A' also motivates people to sign up with their Facebook account or at least link it with their account for better transparency.

This is not all. In case something goes wrong, an insurance policy is available too.

Traveler Retention: Another problem being faced is the retention of travelers. To grow, the company needs to retain its travelers so that they do not choose a hotel on their next vacation. To retain them, it offers promotional codes, and credits to frequent travelers. As a solution to this problem, it also sends such promotions to hosts as to motivate them to take a vacation and stay in a Company 'A' at their favorite destination.

Customer segments

Both the supply as well as the demand side are the customers even though on some platforms only one side pays. On Company 'A' this is clearer as both sides pay. The following are the main segments.

Hosts:

- Hosts are the people who own property and want to make some money by renting out their space.
- They can create a listing for their property on Company 'A', add property details and set their rent, check-in, check-out time, etc.
- Hosts can accept or reject a booking after reading the reviews of the traveler or after going through his social profiles.

Travelers:

- Travelers are the people who book the listed available spaces from local hosts.
- Travelers have the option to search for a property by filtering them according to rent, amenities provided, location, etc.
- Travelers can book a space by paying through the portal.

Freelance Photographers:

- Company 'A' has a vast network of freelance photographers in all major cities of the world who go to a location and click high-definition photographs of the property.
- The high-quality photographs get more responses and the freelance photographers are paid by Company 'A' directly.
- You can segment customers always in different ways depending on the question you are trying to answer. Let's look at some ways of segmenting Company's customers.

Guests:

- By travel type
  - business travel guests; leisure travel
  - tour of multiple destinations; single destination stays
- By demographic
  - single; couple; family with children
  - age brackets
  - pre or post-retirement
- By income bracket
- By interest

Hosts:

- By type of accommodation provided
  - Room; unit/condo; house
  - By home/location
  - Country; city

- By location type
- Countryside; suburb; metropolitan

On the macro level, you can segment

- Rental hosts/guests only
- Event hosts/guests only
- how to make both offerings more complementary (e.g. bundling, discounts, promotions)

These are still very macro segments. All data-driven companies, like Company 'A', create much more micro-segmentation that should be much more valuable than the above traditional segments.

These macro segments can be targeted in various ways: here's an article targeting families with kids and one targeting the post-retirement extensive traveler segment. The articles directly target the respective segments and have links embedded to destination guidebooks and even to listings.

Customer relationships

The most important consideration on this dimension is to firmly own the customer relationship and to keep it within your platform. Company 'A' has poached many customers from Craigslist in their early days. The business travel platforms and Company 'A' will have careful provisions in their contracts and the customer data that they share to avoid "leakages". You might say they are very different platforms but what about losing customers to hotels via the travel platforms or to other short-term rental platforms that may collaborate the travel platform in the future?

Relevant for both sides

- Deal with customer issues inappropriate manner and timeliness. Manage bad behaviors and risks (the "harassing host" and the "house trashing guest") and improve rules continuously
- Transparency around privacy, personal data, etc.
- Portray the desired company image through social and other media

Especially for the hosts

Customer relationships to the supply side (the hosts) is defined by what the platform does for them in terms of income while protecting their property from bad guests.

- The platform's ability to generate continuous income (short gaps between guests, listing up the top ranks, etc.)
- Provide good guests (weed out the bad apples)
- Manage issues (accidents, damages, complaints) swiftly
- Support in the on-boarding process
- Help hosts to succeed in general and
- Help super hosts to stand out and be rewarded

Design your business model

Beyond the customer

There is no field for key stakeholders in the business model. This category is very important for platforms. They are an emerging phenomenon. As such, the public opinion has not yet fully formed, and it will significantly influence your customer's view of your platform.

I have already covered lobbyists and influencers as key partners. But here we need to talk about the public as such.

- Manage the social, communal, economic footprint/impacts of the platform
- Liaise with cities, communities, regulators and other groups as required (and proactively where beneficial)
- Manage the platform's image across the media and other relevant channels
- Manage serious incidents as soon as possible to avoid spreading bad news.

Company 'A' manages several channels through which they publish public opinion influencing articles. They have the Company 'A' newsroom, Company 'A' Citizen and their social media web pages.

Channels

Channels for the awareness and customer acquisition are:

Design your business model

- Digital ad campaigns via different social media websites and apps.
- Content marketing: via their newsroom and guidebooks.
- Word of mouth:

    - Via social media and messaging apps
    - User stories: "our user's stories are more reliable to the market, than our stories"
    - Referral programs rewarding referrer and referral taker with credits
    - Digital influencers

- Free media coverage based on the novelty factor
- Mobile App stores: through high ratings, ads and being featured

Channels for daily transactions:

- Most transactions are fully automated through the app and web pages
- Signing up through the web pages or the app
- Company 'A' uses emails & notifications to engage, stimulate participation, referrals, reinvigorate/recover customers (through special offers, reminders, etc.)
- Keeping existing users engaged and drawing in new users is essential for all businesses. The company's Social media pages are a great example of this.
- Tiered customer support channels

a. Automated customer support for high-volume, low severity issues (e.g. forgotten items) to be rapid

b. Multi-tiered customer support (ability to contact a human) for more severe issues

- Many communication channels, e.g.

  - Company 'A' mag,
  - Company 'A' newsroom,
  - Company 'A' Citizen and them
  - Social Media web pages

Value proposition

Your platform needs to create value for the supply side (hosts) and demand-side (guests) of your platform.

Company 'A' creates value propositions on (at least) three levels (apart from the financial value):

- *Individual connections:* Company 'A' helps to start every guest-host connection on the right foot. Whereas, hotels try to provide the same looks & feel everywhere in the world. Individuality gets lost. The people providing the service must be adjusted to the service delivery standards, etc.
- *Community:* Connections between the users enabled by the vast amounts of user-generated content on the

destination locations as well as the respective accommodation.

- *Localization:* by adding an increasing amount of information/recommendations on the location and adding events provided by event hosts.

This is how the value propositions for the hosts look in more detail:

- Income generation for home repairs to taking a dream trip, hosts use the extra income to fund their passions.
- Ease of transactions:
  1. joining the platform
  2. getting guests
  3. payments, etc.
- Experience of making new friends (if desired)
- Guests are already ID checked, plus the ability to review guests' ratings
- Calendar, booking management through Company 'A'
- Insurance coverage through Company 'A' (hosts still needs insurance for certain items)
- Other host service providers (non-affiliated 3rd parties) from cleaning only to full management

Relevant for both sides:

- Company 'A' recommended hospitality standards
- Responsible hosting guidelines with all tips on safety, hazards, neighbors, etc.

- Dispute resolution process through Company 'A'
- Taking safety and trust seriously

Some of the value propositions for the guests (demand side) are:

- Convenience of booking.
- The amount of choice and variety of types of homes.
- The proposition to experience the destination more authentically.
- Tons of authentic information from locals (hosts) about the destination city (selected large cities).
- Often less expensive than comparable sized hotel rooms.
- Units and especially houses with several bedrooms.
- Cashless transaction.
- Rating system that allows for feedback.

Company 'A' is adding value propositions to both sides that hotels will struggle to compete with. Compare Company 'A' events to the old-fashioned flyers you find in some corner in hotel foyer

Cost structure

Company's most important cost elements are:

- Cost of customer acquisition, CAC: referral credits, digital advertising, paid search, etc.

Design your business model

- The weighted average cost of capital, WACC (can be ~25% for start-ups, for Company 'A' this should be far less)
- Development of new features, ongoing fine-tuning of algorithms, etc.
- Expansion to new cities and new niches
- Payroll for permanent employees and freelancers (e.g. photographers)
- Costs of payment processing
- Lobbying, regulatory compliance
- Legal cases and settlement costs
- Infrastructure costs, computing power, bandwidth
- Customer support
- Insurance, legal costs

I have not distinguished between Capex and Opex, but you can see there are a lot of growth-related costs. The CAPEX components will taper down as the company matures barring, of course, new growth endeavors.

Company 'A' passes some of their costs on to guests/hosts. More on that in a second when we talk about their revenues.

Revenues

Company 'A' offers free listings to property owners and lets travelers browse the listed spaces and select the one which best suits their needs on the platform. The business model of Company 'A' is such that the booking and monetary transactions are done on Company's platform. This is from where the company earns its share of the revenue from 2 different sources which have been explained below:

- *Commission from Property Owners (Hosts)*

Company 'A' charges a flat 10% commission from hosts upon every booking done through the platform.

- *Transaction fee from Travelers (Guests)*

Company 'A' charges 3% of the booking amount as transaction charges from travelers upon every confirmed booking.

On the surface, Company 'A' makes their revenues by charging hosts and guest a service fee per transaction:

- Rental guests pay 5-16%
- Rental hosts pay 3-6%
- Event hosts pay 25%
- Event guests pay 0%

Some short-term rental platforms charge a listing fee rather than per transaction fee. This is a different pricing model.

Here are some interesting observations on the Company's pricing model:

Guests pay 2-3 times higher fees per transaction than hosts. This has to do with supply and demand of hosts and guests and with incentives. Hosts are harder to get as there are

Design your business model

fewer people who have a spare room/unit/house and are willing to rent it out (repetitively) to (potentially untrustworthy) strangers. Guests, by comparison, save money (incentive) compared to hotels.

Hosts pay almost 3% transaction fees if they select a flexible cancellation policy, almost 4% for a moderate and 5% for a strict cancellation policy. They pay more for certainty (though they may miss out on bookings from people who prefer flexibility). If you are offering a vastly popular home, you can more likely afford a strict policy and even pass the additional costs onto the guests by charging a higher price. Company 'A' incentivizes hosts to opt for a more flexible policy as this is the most desirable option from a guest perspective and should lead to more aggregate bookings.

Guest service fees are at the lower end of the 5%-15% range, the higher the overall transaction value. The transaction value is a function of the per night price of the accommodations the duration of the stay. Given guests are already incentivized by low costs, Company 'A' figures they can charge more on the service fee. Another reason, of course, is that fixed costs are roughly the same independent of the accommodation per night price.

- Event fees are very different. There is no service fee for the guest and a 20% service fee for event hosts. Event hosts are easy to get. Many of them have a small local business or a hobby they are good at and use Company 'A' as an additional advertising platform for their offering. No doubt, these people will be quite willing to pay 20% as any booking from Company 'A' is an incremental booking to their other sales channels.

Cost recoveries: Company 'A' passes some of their costs directly onto their customers (beyond operational costs plus margin).

- Company 'A' passes search engine paid search costs onto the hosts whose space is being booked through ads. Host are opted in by default but can opt-out but won't be listed when the potential guests get onto the Company 'A' pages through a paid ad.
- Company 'A' offers professional photography of rental homes in selected cities for a fee.
- There are cleaning (and hosting) service providers for Company 'A' listed properties. These are not affiliated with Company 'A' but promise to comply with the Company 'A' service standards.

Cost comparison hotels vs Company 'A' (cost incentives for guests): There are a lot of interesting financial observations below the surface in online business models, Company 'A' is more complex. Most businesses value proposition is very similar to that of their main competitors. The company's value proposition is more differentiated from traditional hotels. Also, the cost elements and incentives for the participants are different.

Design your business model

One often concludes that price differences vary a lot by city, but that Company 'A' is cheaper in most cities. The study is based on more than 200,000 Company 'A' listing. But there are no further details on their methodology. E.g., have they compared for comparable accommodations or have they just compared the entire inventory across all classes for a given date range? With this caveat, here is the comparison which is decided to take at face value.

Cost base for the hosts: Any revenue consideration needs to consider that the offered accommodation on Company 'A' plus all Company 'A' fees needs to be lower (or at least comparable) to a similar hotel offering. A similar comparison for Company 'A' is much more difficult. Let's still have a brief look.

Look at the different cases of host accommodations, does that make sense

Room: In this case, the hosts rent out one room only. The amenities (kitchen, bathroom, etc.) are shared. The marginal cost for the host is directly correlated to direct costs by the guest, incremental heating, electricity, internet usage, etc. There are two typical cases:

a. The host never had the intention to rent this room out in the classical rental model. In this case, any net income (minus tax) is an additional income. And the host does not even need to worry about how often the room is occupied and can take it how they feel. This is a common cause.

b. If the host has rented the room out permanently before and is keen to obtain a higher income through the Company 'A' model, then the utilization and transaction cost differences play a role. The host will surely be able to get a higher per night rate through Company 'A'. But they will need to do at least a minimum level of servicing of the room themselves after each guest. And they will also have more gaps say over a monthly basis. However, on an annual average basis, things may be different assuming that getting a long-term rental may cause larger gaps in-between tenants. Cost of capital (i.e. pro-rated mortgage interest) needs to be factored in.

Apartment, house: Using the above-mentioned lines of thinking, compare for yourself the case of renting out an entire apartment or house via Company 'A' to renting it out long-term in the classic rental model. There are many considerations and cases. E.g. some people rent out their home while they are on leave themselves (and Company 'A' prompts those who book accommodation through them, to rent out their own space while they are away). Other homeowners rent out individual rooms to different Company 'A' hosts at the same time and so on.

As you can see it is very complex. But Company 'A' needs to understand the above and what motivates hosts to offer their spaces on Company 'A'. It is not all pure financial considerations. And all that I have listed above play a role in motivating hosts.

The question will always be if a platform can create enough cumulative value for its participants so that it can extract enough value for itself. The cost base for the participants (hosts & guests) is at the heart of the revenue question for the platform.

Business model in nutshell

(Online travel accommodation marketplace)

Key Activities	Value Proposition	Customer Segment
• Building traveler's network • Platform development & maintenance • Building host network	**For Hosts** • Easy renting • House insurance • Property maintenance	• Hosts(who rent is house) • Travelers
Key Resources • Technology • Online Platform & Network • Local host & skilled employee		**Customer relationship** • Customer support services • Home insurance • Social media & offers
Key Partners • Host • Guest • Payment processors	**For Guests** • Guest can book homestay instead of hotel • Cheaper accommodation	**Delivery Channels** • Mobile apps & website • Third party logistic

Cost Structure	Revenue Stream
• Payment to employee and freelance • Platform development, maintenance & R&D • Customer support centers	• Commission from host on each booking • Commission from guest on each booking

Design your business model

CHAPTER 10

INNOVATION AND GROWTH

When the winds of change blow, some people build walls and others build windmills
                                        – Chinese proverb

Development of Steam engine technology in Europe is a classic example of innovation in the 16th-18th century. Now steam engines are the great source of power in factories, enabling mass production, and they revolutionized transport with the railways. More recently, information technology transformed the way companies produce and sell their goods and services while opening new markets and new business models.

In simple words, innovation can lead to higher productivity, that means the same input generates a greater output. As productivity rises, more goods and services are produced – with same or even less resources. That translate to the growth of economy. In economic terms, innovation describes the development and application of ideas and technologies that produces better quality of goods and services or make their production cheaper with less manhours.

Managers are trained to make decisions based on available choices. But they don't always have good options. Innovation involves creating new options. This is where designers excel. Apple's extraordinary user experiences were mostly the creation of Jonathan Ive, a professional designer and Jobs' righthand man.

It is important to understand the difference between invention and innovation. Invention is a completely new idea whereas innovation is the commercial application and successful exploitation of the idea.

Fundamentally, innovation means introducing something new to your business. This could be:

- Improving or replacing business processes to increase efficiency and productivity, or to enable the business to extend the range of quality of existing products and/or services
- Developing entirely new and improved products and services - often to meet rapidly changing customer need or consumer demands.
- Value engineering to existing products, services or markets to differentiate the business from its competitors and increase the perceived value by the customers and markets

- Innovation can mean a single breakthrough – e.g. a new product or service. However, it can also be a series of small, incremental changes.
- Innovation is a creative process. The ideas may come from:
a) Inside the business, e.g. from employees, managers or in-house research and development work
b) Outside the business, e.g. suppliers, customers, Competitors, media reports, market research published by another organization, or R&D lab of universities and other sources of new technologies
- Success comes from filtering those ideas, identifying those that the business will focus on and applying resources to exploit them.

Introducing innovation can help you to:

- Improve productivity
- Reduce costs
- Be more competitive
- Build the value of your brand
- Establish new partnerships and relationships
- Increase turnover and improve profitability

Businesses that fail to innovate run on following risk:

- losing market share to competitors
- falling productivity and efficiency
- losing key staff
- experiencing steadily reducing margins and profit
- going out of business

Design your business model

There's no point considering innovation in a vacuum. To grow your business, you must study your marketplace and understand how innovation can add value to your customers.

Unless companies invest in the difficult task of creating new things, they will fail in the future no matter how big their profits remain today. It happens when we've gained everything to fine-tuning the old lines of business that we've inherited. Today's "best practices" will no longer be the best practices of future; the best paths are often new and untried.

Pursuing Business Model Innovation

Business model innovation is one of the most effective ways for companies to stand out from the competition and thus secure the existence of the company, especially in unstable times. Ultimately, it is a matter of breaking down a company into its building blocks, analyzing it and evaluating it, re-inventing them, and, in combination with other, new building blocks, to set them back together systematically.

Product Innovation: This describes the development of a new product, as well as an improvement in the performance or features of an existing product. Mobile companies continued iteration of its smartphones is an example of this.

Process Innovation: Process innovation is the implementation of new or improved production and delivery methods to increase a company's production levels and reduce costs. One of such examples of such innovation is when Ford

Motor Company introduced the first moving assembly line, which shorten the assembly time for a single vehicle down from 12 hours to roughly 90 minutes.

The choice to pursue product, process, or business model innovation will largely depend on the company's competitors, customer and industry. Executives running a product firm, for example, need to constantly think about how they plan to innovate their product.

Some experts say 'When the innovation starts to slow down, that's when firms should be thinking of and looking at next-generation capabilities'

If a company is trying to choose where to focus its efforts for innovation, its business model is the recommended place to start.

Business model innovation is often more impactful on business than product innovations. Now many new business models are disrupting the market. It is significantly more profitable. Changes in customer behavior, globalization and technological innovations are currently creating a "window of opportunity" for new business models.

Attitude to Business Model Innovation

Companies hoping to drive growth through business model innovation face several critical questions: How broad should the scope of the effort be? What's the appropriate level of risk to take? Is it a onetime exercise, or does it call for an ongoing capability?

To answer those questions, it's important to realize that not all business model innovation efforts are alike. Let us have a look at four distinct approaches to business model innovation, which can help executives making effective choices in designing the path to growth:

The reinventor attitude: It is deployed in light of a fundamental industry challenge, such as commoditization or new regulation, in which a business model is deteriorating slowly, and growth prospects are uncertain. In this environment, the company must analyze its customer need and value proposition. The company should align its operations to profitably deliver on the new superior product offering.

The adapter attitude: It is used when the current core business, even if reinvented, is unlikely to combat fundamental disruption. In this situation adapters attitude is the need of hour. The company explore adjacent businesses or markets, in some cases exiting their core business entirely. The company must build an innovation engine to drive experimentation to find a successful "new core" space with the right business model.

The maverick attitude: It deploys business model innovation to scale up a potentially more successful core business. Mavericks are either startups or insurgent established companies, which employ their core advantage to revolutionize or disrupt their industry. To do this, company requires to continually evolve out of the competitive edge, advantage of the business and changing business environment to drive growth.

The adventurer attitude: It aggressively expands the footprint of a business by exploring or venturing into new or adjacent territories. This approach requires an understanding of the company's competitive advantage and placing careful bets on novel applications of that advantage to succeed in new markets.

Some facts about Business Model Innovation

- Each working organization has a business model.
- The business model of a company has to change to ensure its success and, ultimately, its survival.
- The business model is to be seen as a new analysis unit. On the one hand, the focus being on value generation for the customer and on the value recording for the company.
- Business model innovation is the process. It is the result of a change made in the business model. Even minor changes in business model magnifies the benefit to customers and businesses.
- New business models can be deliberately generated. Visualization tools such as the Business Model Canvas support this process.

Design your business model

- Business model is also about experimenting. New business models are not created on the drawing board in isolation with marketplace. It should follow the 'Trial and Error Principle'. We must to the design Prototype testing in the real marketplace and see how it works.

- Business model innovations do not mean a completely new concept. According to the University of St. Gallen, most of business model innovations are new combinations from parts of 'old' or 'other' business models. Therefore, Innovation can be just a combination of already existing ideas.

- Business model innovation should not be seen as a new technology or a new product. Business model innovation, however, is often necessary to generate value from radical product innovation.

- An organization may have a combination of several business models. At the same time, several business models can be successful in one industry.

- Business model innovations have the potential to revolutionize an entire industry.

Business model innovation needs a clear concept. It should facilitate the description and discussion on different aspects of business model building blocks. It has the task of grasping and mediating the basic principle by which a company creates value. Depending on the desired level of detail and abstraction, different concepts are possible. We present here briefly two concepts of different complexity, which, however, fundamentally answer the same questions.

One of the most important benefits of innovation is its contribution to economic growth. Productivity growth brings a lot of benefits for consumers and businesses. As productivity rises, the wages of workers increase. They have more money in their pockets, and so can buy more goods and services. At the same time, businesses become more profitable, which enables them to invest and hire more employees.

The growth companies adopt following best practices:

Find the next S-curve

Nothing grows forever. The best products, markets, and business models go through a predictable growth, which is depicted by S-curve in the business world

Diminishing returns shows that most attractive customers are reached, price competition got tough, the current product loses its glitter and customers are looking for something new and better. It shows customer support challenges emerging and the need of new operating skills seems obvious.

Surprisingly, growth company leaders are often blinded-sided by this predictable speed bump. Once the reality of the S-curve becomes apparent, it is too late to design the next growth strategy, if you haven't already working on future products.

The time to innovate, the first sign appears when the first growth curve hits an inflection point. How do you know when you're hitting the inflection point? You never know. So, the best companies work on present and future product at the same time and make innovation a continuous process.

Steve Jobs understood this when he returned to Apple. In 2002, he challenged his company to break out of the mature computer industry where his company had never garnered much more than 10 percent market share. He told in a *Magazine* interview, "I would rather compete with Sony than ... Microsoft."

Eight years later, when he introduced the iPod, iPhone, iPad, and a game-changing retail channel, he claimed victory and Apple Computer became Apple Inc. While introducing the iPod, he said, "Apple is the largest *mobile devices company* in the world. Larger than the mobile devices businesses of all others coming together."

Lean-to customers

Successful growth companies have a deep understanding of their customers' problems. Many are embracing tools such as the customer empathy map to uncover new opportunities to create value. This customer insight is the foundation for their lean approach to product innovation: rapid prototyping, design partnerships with lead users, and pivoting to improve their product and business model.

It's amazing that few companies invest the time to get out of the office and interact with customers (outside of sales situations). During the turnaround of IBM, Lou Gerstner launched Operation Bear Hug to get the company back in touch with its customers. As per some report, IBM's top 50 executives had to visit five customers per week and deliver a write-up to top management.

Think like a designer

Managers are trained to make choices, but they don't always have enough options. Innovation involves creating new options. This is where designers excel. Apple's exceptional user experiences were largely the creation of a group of professional designers and Jobs' righthand man Jonathan Ive.

Design thinking requires a different set of tools. Growth company strategists have no more interest in Porter's Five Forces Analysis because it assumes that markets have well-defined boundaries and competitors must fight for market share. Instead, they search for blue ocean, an uncontested market space and make competition irrelevant.

Culture of Innovation

Unless the head of business makes innovation a priority, it won't happen. Innovation requires a certain level of risk-taking and failure that's impossible without executive air cover. The growth companies create a culture of innovation:

- When Howard Schultz felt Starbucks had lost its way, he flew in every store manager from all around the world to help redesign its café experience.
- One search engine company encourages its employees to spend one day per week on new ideas.
- Consumer goods company tracks the percentage of revenues from new products and services.
- One Advertising company gives a Heroic Failure Award to the riskiest ideas ... that fail!

More important are innovative leaders as role models. Amazon founder Jeff Bezos has told both employees and partners that he cares less about profitability and more about planting seeds that are likely to pay off in five to seven years. He's so driven by the vision that he's investing over $40 million of his own money in a product designed to last for 10,000 years.

To launch his successful Think Different campaign, Steve Jobs commissioned *The Crazy Ones*, a video that featured Einstein, Edison, Gandhi, Muhammad Ali, Hitchcock, Richard Branson, and other "trouble-makers" who changed the world. Employee understood the CEO's views on risk-taking and innovation.

Adopting following four practices can help any company drive innovation and growth.

Business growth can be achieved either by boosting the top line with greater product sales or service income or by increasing the bottom line or profitability of the operation by minimizing costs.

Why business needs more experimentation

Big businesses typically introduce large new interventions without prior small-scale testing. They rarely trial them out at a small scale, evaluate the different options, and then scale up those that work.

The result is that we put billions in schemes to support innovation, entrepreneurship, and growth, yet we don't know what works and what doesn't. We are probably wasting resources on ineffective schemes while depriving funding to those that would make a difference.

Experimental approach in business is also important in an ever-changing world. We cannot assume that the same old instruments continue to be the best tools to support innovation and growth if they ever were. The environment keeps changing. New challenges emerge. But also new opportunities for tackling them.

We need to take advantage of these to try out new ways to support innovation and growth, whether testing small tweaks to existing programs or experimenting with radically novel types of schemes.

Design your business model

Ultimately, innovating in the design of the programs and institutions that help make our countries more innovative and entrepreneurial is crucial to increasing economic growth and addressing the societal challenges that we face.

Managing Business Growth

Business owners generally love the word "growth" since when used concerning a business, it usually means success. A growing business seems thriving business, or so most of us believe. Unfortunately, many small business owners find it hard way that business growth may result in problems if your business isn't equipped to handle that growth - and can even kill your business altogether!

All growing businesses eventually reach their limit. You might run out of resources to handle the new volume of orders or customers. You might not have sufficient product to meet demand. Most small businesses struggle to manage operational issues during a growth phase, and it can be hard to decide whether it's time to hire additional employees or if this is just a short-term growth in sales or customer volume. The following are tips for managing growth in business.

Role of Management

If you find yourself doing the tasks of your employees - creating the products or fulfilling the services your company offers, it's time to take a step back. As the business owner, you must maintain a management role in the organization. If you don't have enough manpower without you on the front lines, it's time to either replace existing employees who are not generating the necessary return on investment (what you pay them), or hire additional employees so that you may focus on the administration, management, and strategy.

Define Systems and Procedures

When a business is started, many small business owners do the quality check over their employee's work, correct any mistakes or problems before they reach the customer, and generally just keep a close eye on how everything is running. If you are growing rapidly, you won't have the time to continue this with as much detail. A business needs systems and procedures in place for managing staff and providing the products or services of the company. There should be product or service quality control standards to ensure the business produces the same level quality whether you are in a slow period or a growth period. You should look at your daily business operations and determine what tasks can follow specific systems and procedures, and then get everyone on board. When your business relies on systems and procedures, it will manage growth much better than one that simply scrambles to keep up as business expands.

Keeping Growth in Check

For business owners, growth is welcomed but it's important to keep your growth in check. When you start generating more cash than you had previously, it can be tempting to spend more money than you're able to - perhaps you decide to upgrade computer or technology or hire more staff to handle the business growth. Both are excellent uses of business income, but if you're not careful you may spend more than you can afford and then your financial stability could be compromised. The growth phase that is expected to be resulted in higher profits could easily turn around and cause a cash flow problem if you aren't careful to keep the growth of the business in check.

Business Growth is a stage where the business reaches the point for expansion and seeks additional options to generate more profit. Business growth is depending on the business lifecycle, industry growth trends, and the owners desire for equity value creation.

Business growth capital is very critical for all scale-up minded businesses. Choosing the right business growth capital for the business takes expertise and market knowledge- as no two companies are the same. Choose correctly, and your growth takes off. Choose unwisely and it could be a disaster. Rather than fit your capital need to a pre-existing structure, smart companies design their structure to mitigate risk. Business growth is a function of resource availability and often requires an upfront investment. Whether an acquisition or business investment, it pays to be conservative in projecting returns over time. Choosing the right business growth capital depends on following variables:

- The size of the capital raise.
- The cost of capital
- The flexibility of capital.
- The term structure of capital.

Design your business model

These four variables must be optimized to arrive at the best solution. Most companies use an advisor to evaluate and source capital, due to the criticality of the job. Each of these variables is solved with market intelligence and deal-making expertise. The result is a business growth capital solution that satisfies your unique need and allows your scale-up vision to take flight.

Planning a Growth Strategy

Market Penetration. The least risky growth strategy for any business is to simply sell more of its current product to its current customers-; a strategy perfected by large consumer goods companies, says McFarland. Think of how you might buy a six-pack of beverages, then a 10-pack, and then a case. "You can't even buy toilet paper in less than a 24-roll pack these days," McFarland jokes. Finding new ways to utilize your product for customer; like turning baking soda into a deodorizer for your refrigerator; is another form of market penetration.

Market Development. The next rung up the ladder is to devise a way to sell more of your current product to an adjacent market-; offering your product or service to customers in another city or state, for example. Experts points out that many of the great fast-growing companies of the past few decades relied on Market Development as their main growth strategy. For example, Express Personnel (also called Express Employment Professionals), a staffing business that began in Oklahoma City quickly opened offices around the country via a franchising model. Eventually, the company offered employment staffing services in some 588 different locations, and the company became the fifth-largest staffing company in the U.S.

Alternative Channels. This growth strategy involves pursuing customers differently such as, for example, selling your products online. When Apple added its retail division, it was also adopting such strategy. Using the Internet as a channel for your customers to access your products or services in a new way, such as by adopting a rental model or software as a service, is another Alternative Channel strategy.

Product Development. A classic strategy, new products are developed to sell to your existing customers as well as to new ones. If it is possible, you would ideally like to sell your new products to existing customers. Because selling products to your existing customers is far less risky than "having to learn a new product and market at the same time," expert says.

New Products for New Customers. Sometimes, changing market conditions dictate that you must create new products for new customers, as Polaris, the recreational vehicle manufacturer in Minneapolis found out. For years, the company produced only snowmobiles. Then, after many mild winters, the company was in dire straits. At the same time, it developed a wildly successful series of four-wheel all-terrain vehicles with an entirely new market. Apple pulled off the similar strategy when it introduced the iPod. What made the iPod such a breakthrough product was that it could be sold alone, without an Apple computer, but, at the same time, it also exposes more new customers to the computers Apple offered. Expert says the iPhone has had a similar impact; once customers started enjoying the look and feel of the product's, they opened themselves up to buying other Apple products.

If you choose to follow one of the Intensive Growth Strategies, you should ideally take only one step up the ladder at a time, since each step brings risk, uncertainty, and effort. Sometimes, the market forces you to take action as a means of self-preservation, as it did with Polaris. Sometimes, you have no choice but to take more risk, says McFarland.

You must Know what you do and what you don't

Some of the best advice I learned early on was don't try to be all things to all people, because it typically means you are not very good at any one thing. It is a mistake to take on far-reaching service offerings, develop products outside your comfort zone or expand outside of your target markets just to make a few extra bucks. When you do that, you jeopardize your core strength to focus on what you may not be successful at and create unnecessary pressures for your team, your budgets, and your company as a whole.

Product differentiation and product diversification

Product differentiation: A product is a bundle of potential benefits offered to a purchaser. However, certain products basically look alike. Take toothpaste, for example. These are produced by different manufacturers and were it not for the tube and the branding, the customer would not even be able to distinguish between the products of most different manufacturers. To make their product distinct from others the manufacturers identify them to the customer, that is, `differentiate', by using different packaging, coloring, etc. and by emphasizing different benefits or advantages in their promotion. All products do not appeal to all income groups or age groups unless they are meant to satisfy necessities. A manufacturer can use the need-oriented segmentation. For example, a toothpaste manufacturer may appeal to the prevention of `tooth decay', while another might offer `sociability' in the sense of preventing bad breath. Still, another may provide the need to be `attractive' by emphasizing the whiteness of the teeth which his product, toothpaste, give. This lathe concept of product positioning. Thus, positioning is used for creating differentiation in a manufacturer's product.

Product Diversification: As soon as a manufacturer offers more than one product, it is described as product diversification. Generally, diversification is categorized into two types:

- Related Diversification and
- Unrelated Diversification.

Where the new products introduced in the product mix are similar to the existing product, this diversification is described as 'related'. When a company accepts new products, which are very different from the existing products, this diversification is said to be `unrelated'.

Related Diversification

Related diversification is the commonest form of diversification, inexpensive and easier. diversification in each Product Line. These also constitute a Product Line. We can also include a different variety of passenger cars manufactured by a company as part of a related diversification strategy.

However, relatedness is sometimes stretched to include other similar items. For example, two different kinds of toothpaste brands from the same company.

Probable reasons for companies undertaking related diversification are:

- To make more effective use of the existing selling and distribution facilities,
- To use its under-utilized production capacity,
- To meet varied customer needs,
- To take advantage of its existing brand in a particular type of products, and
- To grow the sale of existing products.
- By putting the product in varied price range and variety, companies create tough competition for newcomers and competitors.

Unrelated Diversification

When the new products introduced are quite different from the existing ones, the company is said to have adopted the strategy of unrelated diversification. For example, if a consumer products' manufacturer diversifies into the manufacture of raw materials such as chemicals or industrial products, such diversifications are unrelated diversification. This involves heavier costs and management challenges. This is the reason why related diversification is more popular

Stay focused on the prize

We have always tried to be strategic in our approach to growth. We set multi-year business plans, track against those plans, and modify them when necessary. If you don't set goals you have no way of measuring yourself, your team and your company against some pre-determined objectives. When everyone understands in a very crystal-clear way what the overall goals of the organization are, it allows everyone to rally together and take pride in accomplishing them.

People work for people, not companies

It is rare when a business can successfully operate and grow without talented people. We often talk about our people being the only asset we have to sell, and we are always looking for ways to improve our culture, our benefits, and the reasons why employees would want to keep working for us. Many companies forget that true loyalty comes when employees believe that the organization and its leadership team care about them personally and professionally. This finally results in long-tenured employees, which has a very real and direct effect on company growth.

Running a company well is different than being good at a trade or profession

I have often said that just because someone is good at PR, it doesn't mean they will be good at running a PR agency. The same is true for any profession. Growing a successful business is all about having a good business mindset, combined with a strong skillset in your particular area of expertise. The behind-the-scenes type of business--such as process, people management, billing, and operations--are very critical to business success. I have seen several very smart people get into business only to ultimately fail because they didn't look at their business through the lens of operational success, and instead focused only on being good at their profession.

Passion is contagious

If you are passionate in what you do it shows to the people surrounding you every day in the office, facility or production plant. Showing enthusiasm cannot be underscored enough in terms of how it relates to the team working harder, being more focused, and ultimately more successful at their job. This translates to a better end-product. The opposite can be said for someone who is not happy, leads through negative motivation, creates a challenging work environment and doesn't love what they do.

Challenge yourself to always keep improving

Technology is changing the world we live in every day. To stay relevant and fresh, it is important to innovate, regardless of your industry, as well as want to get better. This could mean new programs, new technology, new thinking or new processes. I believe there is no place for stagnant, you are either moving forward or you are becoming obsolete. We are constantly looking at our way of doing things and looking for ways to improve our end product, improve our client relations skills, and become more efficient at what we do, which ultimately drives greater profitability.

"Build it and they will come" mentality Doesn't work

During a turbulent economy, many brands look at marketing as an expense and therefore try to cut it from the budget. However, the marketplace is filled with good ideas that lacked the marketing support to gain traction or they were launched with the ideology of "our product is so great, that consumers will flock to it." Consumers are incredibly discerning about their money; as a result, they buy products that they have either sampled or have been referred to them. Therefore, make sure that marketing is aligned with product innovation and roll-out to ensure that when the product is ready for retail consumption strong consideration has been given to how the product will be marketed.

Unfortunately, there is no guarantee for business success. It takes a combination of strategic logic and creative thinking to ensure that a brand or business is successful. However, the aforementioned recommendations will help alleviate some of the common pitfalls that many businesses face as they look to gain traction and acceptance.

A story on the business model innovation

The construction of engines for a British aircraft turbine manufacturer was exclusively a product business: For a comparatively large one-off sum, the engine became the property of the aircraft manufacturers.

They introduced a business model innovation. The new business model does not sell engines but thrust hours to the airlines. The airlines pay only for the operating hours of the engines and are no longer obliged to buy the turbine engines. The engine remains the property of Rolls-Royce, and the company is also responsible for the maintenance and repair of the engines.

This business model is based on a performance-based contracting approach, i.e. performance-related remuneration. It is not the value of the engines per sell that is calculated, but the flight performance hours that can be achieved with the engine. Cost factors such as operation, maintenance, and repair are already included in the price. With this innovation, this British aircraft turbine manufacturer has not only created advantages for itself and its customers but also made it possible for low-cost airlines.

If you look at business model innovation from the perspective of the Business Model building blocks,

- There are almost no changes in value creation side (Key activity, key resources & key partners)
- No changes in value delivery side (Customer segment, customer relationship & channel)
- No changes in cost structure
- Changes are made in value proposition which impacts revenue steam of the company.

CHAPTER 11

CALIBRATE AND ALIGN

The measure of intelligence is the ability to change something.

The days when companies could plan more than 5 years are far behind us. Even those markets that used to be incredibly stable, aren't so anymore. New technologies offer opportunities, disruptive innovations pose threats to the existing businesses. That makes it important for companies to stay in the loop. Calibration method ensures you will remain on the right track, by examining your vision and strategy in the light of actual performance, facts, and trends. Calibration is briefly described as an activity where the instrument being tested is compared to a known reference value. At the simplest level, calibration is a comparison between measurements – one of known magnitude or correctness made or set with one set with another set of goal targeted. All the businessman does the same thing in a

Design your business model

nutshell: Plan your business, but things at the place as per your business model, set goals, take action and continuously calibrate towards better results in line with set goals.

How would you know how well your business is doing (or how poorly) if you don't track your results and progress? To calibrate, the 1st step is to measure the performance. How you can measure the performance of your business? There are many indicators or measurements, which indicates how you are performing. For example, it can be net profit, Sales, profit margin, etc.

For a small business with few resources, it is not wise to perform measurement of so many indicators. Here you can use 80/20 rule, which is also called the *"Pareto Principle."* It was named after its founder, the Italian economist Vilfredo Pareto, back in 1895.

What is 80/20 rule?: Pareto found that people in society seemed to divide naturally into what he called the *"vital few,"* or the top 20 percent in terms of money and influence, and the other group is *"trivial many,"* or the bottom 80 percent.

Later, he found that virtually all economic activity was subject to this principle, in that 80 percent of the wealth of Italy during that time was controlled by 20 percent of the population.

We can take Pareto's 80/20 rule and apply it to almost any situation in life. Understanding the principle is important to learning how to prioritize your tasks, days, weeks, and months.

Using the 80/20 principle you can find out the most important 20% key performance Indices (KPI), which indicates 80% of business performance.

How to apply the 80 / 20 Rule in Goal Setting?

Here's what you should do to effectively apply the 80/20 rule to setting SMART goals which will boost your overall productivity.

First, take a piece of paper and write down ten indicators. Then ask yourself: *If you could only measure one of the indicators on that list for your business performance measure, which one indicator would you like to measure?*

Then pick the second most important indicator. What you'll find is, after you complete this exercise, you will have determined the most important 20 percent of your KPI's that will help you to measure your business performance more than anything else.

Let us see in detail, what KPI means to a business

A Key Performance Indicator (KPI) is a measurable value that demonstrates how effectively a business is achieving key business objectives. business use KPIs at multiple levels to evaluate their success at reaching targets. High-level KPIs

Design your business model

may focus on the overall performance of the company, while low-level KPIs may focus on processes in departments such as sales, marketing, HR, service and others. For a small business, we may have very few overall KPIs.

To evaluate the relevance of a performance indicator is to use the SMART criteria. The letters (S-M-A-R-T) are typically taken to stand for Specific, Measurable, Attainable, Relevant, Time-bound. In other words:

- Is your objective **S**pecific?
- Can you **M**easure progress towards that business goal?
- Is the business goal realistically **A**ttainable?
- How **R**elevant is the goal of your business?
- What is the **T**imeframe for achieving this goal?

Once KPI is there and measurement is done. We can analyze the data to know how your business is performing. Now the calibration comes into the picture. If you find that business is not performing on some specific component of business canvas, it is time to look at that and calibrate by taking corrective actions. It may be possible that all components of the business canvas are working fine but we may have a problem in the integration, or we may have some issues with the business model. You may need to calibrate the business model, in the light of the present situation, competition or some other factors.

The analysis of KPI measurement data will give you important insights into the following important questions.

Design your business model

- What worked well in the last quarter? (Note: Do more of that!)
- What didn't work and why?
- What can you do differently in your business?
- What goals would you like your business to reach in the next six months/one year?
- Where do you see your business in the next three years?

Focus on the short-term goals, but also plan for the long game. If you're using a business dashboard, that can make it easier to see how your actual performance compared to your projections and model possible future scenarios.

You also update the business model in specific situations as follows:

New Revenue Opportunities

The company's business model specifies what are the target customer segments. Marketing strategies are then formulated to reach these groups and persuade them to purchase from the company. New revenue opportunities often emerge as the company's business model proves to be successful. Management discovers that the products or services created for one group may be useful for these other groups as well. The business model is modified and expanded to include the new markets the company intends to reach.

Design your business model

Change in Competitive Environment

A business model is designed to help a company build a competitive advantage. Competitors respond by constructing their models to create their advantages. When an old model puts a business in an unfavorable competitive position, it has to be changed. This could involve a radical change such as discontinuing a product line that is no longer selling well, or it could be a matter of adding elements to the value proposition, so the customers perceive they are getting more for their money than they did before.

An often-overlooked element in a good business is a thorough analysis of competitors.

You can learn a lot from watching your competitors. Competitor data allows you to see what they are doing, so you can decide if you should do the same or take a different approach, which wins over your competitor. If competitors are doing something that works, consider copying them.

Get valuable insight into how your competitors are marketing their products, who their target audience is, and what makes them unique.

Online Search engine is always a good starting point. Getting ahold of your competitor's marketing material is another. If you come across a competitor's customers, take a moment to ask them why they chose to do business with your competition. By studying your competition, you may be able to find few ideas to help grow your business.

The Industry Is Changing

Sometimes, external forces that you have no control over can influence your business. If the industry you work in is changing remarkably, this may prompt you to change your business model as well.

Online and technology-based industries are constantly changing that is why you must keep up with the curve and diversify your business.

The way you made huge success and the bulk of your income last year could be a declining trend this year. You may find that your business has more competition now and needs to set a new trend to bring in customers. This could involve taking big moves like discontinuing a product line, adding a new product or service, or enhancing the value you can provide. For example, the rise of e-commerce is mostly due to change in the channel they are connecting with the customer, which is the online way. Now a customer needs to visit a shop to see the items which he wants to purchase. Even he can order his shopping and pay on delivery. These are simply changed in business models, by innovating its building blocks.

The costs and risks of not calibrating

Unfortunately, calibration has costs associated with it and in uncertain economic times, this activity can often become neglected or the interval between calibration checks on instruments can be extended to cut costs or simply through a scarcity of resources or manpower. Neglecting calibration can lead to unscheduled production or machine downtime, product and process quality issues or even product recalls and rework. Furthermore, if the instrument is critical to a processor is located in a hazardous area, allowing that sensor to drift over time could potentially result in a risk to employee safety. Similarly, an end product manufactured by a company with poorly calibrated instruments could present a risk to both consumers and customers. In certain situations, this may even lead to a company losing its license to operate due to the company not meeting its regulatory requirements. This is particularly true for the food and beverage sector and pharmaceutical manufacturers. Weighing instruments must be calibrated regularly. Determining the correct mass of a product is particularly important for companies that supply steel, paper and pulp, power, aviation companies, harbors, and retail outlets, who invoice customers based on the mass of what they supply. These companies have to prove not only that the mass is accurate but also that the equipment producing the readings was correctly calibrated. Invoicing in such industries is often based on process measurements. There is, therefore, a growing need to have the metrological quality of these weighing instruments confirmed by calibration. Product manufacturing also depends on accurate masses and so laboratories and production departments in certain sectors like the food and beverage, oil and gas, energy, chemicals, and pharmaceuticals industries, also need to calibrate their weighing instruments.

Calibration is equally important to measure KPIs to insure, if it is on track or not

Alignment for Fit of your calibrated Business Model Building Blocks

You must achieve a fit of the different business model bricks of your company. It means that the 9 building blocks of your business should be mutually reinforcing and form a coherent whole. After calibration, you have to look at it for a coherent whole once again. For example, you must find the best distribution channels to deliver your value proposition. But when you have found those channels you must ask yourself what the best distribution channel design is for your specific customer segmentation. Then you must go on and ask yourself what kind of customer relationship you should build up with these customers for your particular value proposition and how your distribution channels can support this. Once you have designed these customer-facing aspects of your business model you have to go on and achieve a fit with the infrastructure-related aspects of your business model. You must ask yourself what kind of activities you have to perform to deliver your value proposition? What kind of resources and capacities do you need to build the customer relationships your business model requires? What kind of partnerships make sense to leverage your business? And finally, all this has to fit together in cost structures and a revenue model that allows you to maintain a healthy profit. That's basic business model alignment.

Design your business model

Alignment for Positioning of your updated Business Model in the Environment and Competition

The second level of alignment is with the business model environment and competitive landscape. What sense would it make to have a business model with neatly fitting building blocks that can't withstand the stiff wind of competition? Having a business model that is aligned with competitors means understanding the competitive environment and designing your business model accordingly. It also means to align according to the modifications made during calibration in Business model to meet the current environment and competition. In the 90s Dell computers understood how selling computers through direct-to-customer channels could disrupt the business models of its competitors. When Compaq (now HP) tried to follow Dell indirectly selling to its customers they didn't realize that their business model was neither aligned internally nor with the marketplace. Because they traditionally sold through resellers they couldn't switch to direct channels because their resellers would threaten them with drastic sanctions. More broadly your business model should be aligned with calibrations in 5 forces of your business model environment: Technology, Competition, Customer Demand, Social Environment, and the Legal Environment.

Alignment for updated Business Model with Future Scenarios

Good companies are those that have a business model with a perfect fit and a strong competitive position in the market.

Great companies are those that have a portfolio of business models that are ready for the future. The music industry, for instance, is an example of what can happen when you are badly aligned with possible futures. The major record companies were taken by surprise when illegal trading platforms allegedly stole a large portion of their growth & market. Yet, one could argue that they were simply too lazy to align their traditional business model with the realities and opportunities of the digital age. They were too late in trying to figure out how their current business models would perform in the future.

In terms of alignment this means that if you want to move from competition to future scenarios, you have to try to understand how the 5 forces of your business model environment could evolve in the future. You should reflect on how technology, competition, customers, industry, society and laws will change and what possible impact this could have on your current business model. There are many different techniques to evaluate possible futures, such as scenario planning, prediction markets, systems dynamics and so on. All you need to do is to map these possible outcomes of an uncertain future back to your current business model to be better prepared for the rough days ahead of you.

A story on being responsive to the trends and business environment

One Camera making company had the first digital camera back in the seventies. Whenever technology changes the landscape of an industry, some businesses adapt and Thrive and others that continue doing the same old thing until it's too late. The camera making company who fell behind due to the advent of the digital camera. The situation was a little different, this company patented the first digital camera back in the seventies. It was one that used a magnetic cassette to store images of about a hundred kilobytes. However, over the coming years, this company made so much money of film, that they let the technology gather dust not realizing it's potential. The company continued to focus on traditional film cameras, even when it was clear that the market was moving towards digital. when This camera making company finally got into the digital Market, they were selling cameras at a loss and still couldn't make up enough sales to catch up with those competitors which had seen the potential of digital cameras early on. Currently, the company is losing heavily each year. So, the lesson learned in the world of business is: always keep an eye on the market, see the trends early, be responsive to Future Trends and be innovative. If not, it could cost you everything

Design your business model